GREAT WAR BRITAIN

BIRMINGHAM

Remembering 1914–18

SIAN ROBERTS

IN ASSOCIATION WITH THE LIBRARY OF BIRMINGHAM

The
History
Press

This book is dedicated to the memory of Pam Gwynfa Williams –
Birmingham teacher, historian and friend.

First published 2014

The History Press
The Mill, Brimscombe Port
Stroud, Gloucestershire, GL5 2QG
www.thehistorypress.co.uk

British Library Cataloguing in Publication Data.
A catalogue record for this book is available from the British Library.

ISBN 978 0 7509 5969 8

Typesetting and origination by The History Press
Printed in Malta by Melita Press.

CONTENTS

TIMELINE

1914

28 June

Assassination of Archduke Franz Ferdinand in Sarajevo

4 August

Great Britain declares war on Germany

23 August

Battle of Tannenberg commences

29 August

Lord mayor offers to raise Birmingham City Battalion

1 September

First wounded arrive at 1st Southern General Hospital

4 September

The first Belgian refugees arrive in Birmingham

6 September

First Battle of the Marne

19 October

First Battle of Ypres

1915

25 April

Allied landing at Gallipoli

7 May

Germans torpedo and sink the Lusitania

28 May

Highbury Hospital opens in Joseph Chamberlain's former home

31 May

First German Zeppelin raid on London

28 June

Birmingham's first VC awarded to Herbert James

20 December

Allies finish their evacuation of and withdrawal from Gallipoli

1916

24 January

The British Government introduces conscription

21 February

Battle of Verdun commences

31 May

Battle of Jutland

4 June

Brusilov Offensive commences

1 July

First Day of the Battle of the Somme, 57,000 British casualties

27 August

Italy declares war on Germany

29 September

Opening of Birmingham Municipal Bank

18 December

Battle of Verdun ends

1917

6 April

The United States declares war on Germany

9 April

Battle of Arras

14 May

Appointment of Birmingham's first women police officers

31 July

Third Battle of Ypres (Passchendaele)

20 August

Third Battle of Verdun

26 October

Second Battle of Passchendaele

20 November

Battle of Cambrai

7 December

The United States declares war on Austria-Hungary

12 December

General rationing of food introduced in Birmingham

31 December

Tank Bank Week begins in Birmingham

1918

3 March
Russia and the Central Powers sign the Treaty of Brest-Litovsk

21 March
Second Battle of the Somme

15 July
Second Battle of the Marne

8 August
Battle of Amiens, first stage of the Hundred Days Offensive

21 September
Birmingham Win the War Day

22 September
The Great Allied Balkan victory

27 September
Storming of the Hindenburg Line

8 November
Armistice negotiations commence

9 November
Kaiser Wilhelm II abdicates, Germany is declared a Republic

11 November
Armistice Day, cessation of hostilities on the Western Front

1919

6 January
Farewell event for Birmingham's Belgian refugees

1925

4 July
Opening of Birmingham's Hall of Memory

ACKNOWLEDGEMENTS

I would like to thank all my colleagues in the Learning Resources Team of the Library of Birmingham for their help and support, particularly Charlotte Tucker and Kathryn Hall from the Digital Team and Nhia Huynh from the Conservation Team. Grateful thanks are also due to Anne Elliott from the Music Library for the information about music in the period, to Dr Andy Green for his initial research in the newspaper collections, and to Professor Ian Grosvenor with whom I have collaborated on the research into children during the war.

I am grateful to Sarah Foden and the Cadbury Archive, Mondelēz International for permission to reproduce the images on pages 35, 110, 140 and 144, and to Jo-Ann Curtis and Birmingham Museums Trust for access to the oral histories at the museum and permission to quote from the interviews. I would also like to thank the Barrow family for their kind permission to reproduce the two illustrations by Joseph Southall.

INTRODUCTION

'Sorrow seems on every hand.'

Elizabeth Cadbury, August 1916

'Do we realise what historic times these are?'

Henry Gibbs, January 1919

The two voices above both appear in the First World War archives of the Library of Birmingham. Both represent different experiences of living through the conflict in the city. Elizabeth Cadbury, an affluent and privileged woman of influence, who would later be honoured for her part in the war effort, was writing during the summer of the Somme. The second writer, Henry Gibbs, was a boy just turning 14, reflecting on the advent of peace and the last four and a half years of his childhood a few days before he left school.[1]

The First World War touched the lives of every man, woman and child in Birmingham. All aspects of life were affected – from the price of food, to family life and a child's education at school. How an individual experienced the conflict, however, was profoundly coloured by age, gender, social class, nationality, and economic circumstances. A person's religious beliefs or political perspective could radically determine the choices they made or the paths they followed. For some the war brought a chance to expand their horizons: to serve their country, learn new skills or earn higher wages, even if these opportunities were only temporary. For others the war brought permanent change, fracturing their world through death, disability or grief for the loss of loved ones.

This book aims to tell some of the stories of how war was experienced by people in Birmingham, as told through the city's archive collections. It is not intended as a complete history of the city and its people at war as that would be far too large a task for one book. The first history of Birmingham and the war was published by Brazier and Sandford in 1921, and for several aspects of the conflict it remains the standard reference work. With the notable exception of Terry Carter's *Birmingham Pals*, many aspects of Birmingham and the First World War remain largely under researched and untold.

One of the aims of this book, therefore, is to draw attention to the potential riches of the Library of Birmingham's archive and local history collections, and encourage people to use them to explore the history of their families or local communities during the conflict. It also hopefully brings to the fore some of the lesser-known aspects of Birmingham at war, such as the experience of children, the tensions and issues faced by families, and the real dilemmas faced by individuals as they responded to circumstances that are hard for us, a century later, to comprehend.

All the images, and the vast majority of the quotations from archives used in this book, come from the collections of the Library of Birmingham unless stated otherwise. Document reference numbers are given in the endnotes to each chapter, and the original spelling and punctuation has been retained when quoting from archive sources.

Sian Roberts, Collection Curator,
Library of Birmingham, 2014

Endnotes

1   MS 466/1/1/15/3/13; *The Cradle*, January 1919.

1

MOBILISING THE CITY

Birmingham at the outbreak of war was a leading city of the British Empire, where huge wealth and opportunity sat side by side with extreme poverty and hardship. It had grown dramatically from the small town of the eighteenth century to a manufacturing and industrial powerhouse, and the major employers – Cadbury, Dunlop, Nettlefold and Austin – employed thousands of workers. Granted city status in 1889, it was then expanded considerably by the Greater Birmingham Act of 1911 which almost trebled the city's geographical area and brought Aston Manor, Erdington, Handsworth, Yardley and most of King's Norton and Northfield within the city boundary. A month before war was declared, on 2 July 1914, the city's best-known politician and elder statesman, Joseph Chamberlain, died and was buried at Key Hill Cemetery.

Even before the war began, the impact of European uncertainty was felt in Birmingham. The end of July and first few days of August 1914 saw a significant rise in the cost of living as food prices rocketed. On Saturday, 31 July the price of butter, bacon and sugar went up alarmingly.[1] A few days later the local press reported a run on food shops and many closed their premises.[2] By the end of the first week of war, the price of sugar had increased from two and a half pence a pound to between five and six pence, and bacon from between ten pence and one shilling per pound to over a shilling and two pence a pound. Some of the immediate wartime measures made the situation worse,

Playbill from the Gaiety Theatre advertising a war news film, August 1914.
(Theatre Playbills Collection)

the military requisitioning of forty-five of the Co-operative Society's horses, for example, meant that routine food deliveries were impossible.

The hike in prices was accompanied by a depression in trade. Contracts and orders were cancelled or put on hold due to uncertainty about the situation. Countless people were made unemployed or put on short time which dramatically affected their pay. Firms such as Tangye, Metropolitan Waggon Works and many of the jewellery firms made drastic reductions to the working week, down to half time in many cases. William Henry Norton worked in the stores department at Veritys Plume and Victoria Works in Aston. On 7 August he received a letter from the firm:

> Owing to the war ... an immediate reduction in expenses is necessitated. Able-bodied unmarried men will not be required, as such can go to the Front and fight for their Country and homes, while the services of most of the lady members of the staff will be dispensed with temporarily; others will be put on reduced pay. In your case your salary will be reduced by 50% as from Monday, August 17th. If the war continues further reductions may be necessary.[3]

The local labour exchange dealt with double the normal rates of unemployment. In July 1914 there were 2,600 men and 600 women registered as unemployed. By the end of August this had increased to 6,200 men and 1,700 women. Male unemployment reduced during September and there were fewer than 4,000 men registered by the end of the month. In contrast the number of unemployed women increased to 1,766. Although the problems were short term and industry and employment would see a recovery very soon, there is no doubt that it caused significant hardship, particularly to the poorest who had no savings on which to fall back and so had to turn to charities for help. The records of the children's charity Middlemore Emigration Homes illustrate how the outbreak of the war affected the poorest, and those whose circumstances as single or widowed parents exacerbated their difficulties. On 28 September, George Ball, a single father who worked at Brotherton & Co. in Nechells, turned to Middlemore for help when he could no longer maintain his child on his own. His earnings – twenty-two shillings a week when in full-time employment – had decreased substantially and he was in considerable debt. Similarly, in November, Ellen Elsmore – a single mother and hand-press worker – reported that her weekly earnings were normally between nine and twelve shillings but for the previous several weeks she had been paid only seven shillings a week and, as her rent alone was three and six, she had fallen into arrears.[4]

Great hardship was also caused in the early weeks of the war by the failure of the army to pay the separation allowance (a financial support due to the wives and dependants of soldiers who had enlisted) on time. Local schools reported an immediate effect on children in the poorer parts of the city as families who had lost a wage earner struggled to make ends meet. On 24 August 1914, Mr Tipper, the head teacher of Dartmouth Street School, recorded in his logbook that 'Owing to the War there is much distress in this district. About 40 fathers and 60 brothers of our boys have been called up. The number of Free Brk. [breakfast] Cases has risen from 30 to 70. Next week will see it doubled.' The numbers peaked on 25 September, when 300 boys were receiving free breakfasts at school. By mid-October the separation payments were beginning to come through and the hardship cases decreased accordingly.[5]

The initial distress caused by the war was so intense that a meeting of social welfare workers from across the city was called at the instigation of the acting lord mayor, Alderman Bowater, on 7 August. They formed the Birmingham Citizens' Committee, which brought together the existing charitable provision of the City Aid Society and the Birmingham branch of the Charity Organisation Society. The Citizens' Committee's function was to relieve distress and administer national relief funds such as the Prince of Wales' Fund. Bowater also launched a public appeal to raise money. The Citizens' Committee comprised of a central committee based at the Council House and forty-one district committees across the city. It made temporary grants to those in need of relief and assisted with managing unemployment through a scheme for transferring people who had been thrown out of work in one trade to another where there was a labour shortage. Women, who formed a substantial part of the unemployed, were transferred from occupations such as dressmaking, tailoring, the cycle trade and pen-making into munitions and other war-related work. As government war contracts began to come through the situation improved; by the end of March 1915 there were only 249 cases of unemployment on the books.

Recruiting Office at the Municipal Technical School, c. 1914. (MS 4616/1)

RECRUITING OFFICE
WANTED 500,000 MEN
GOD SAVE THE KING
HEAD QUARTERS NATIONAL RESERVE.

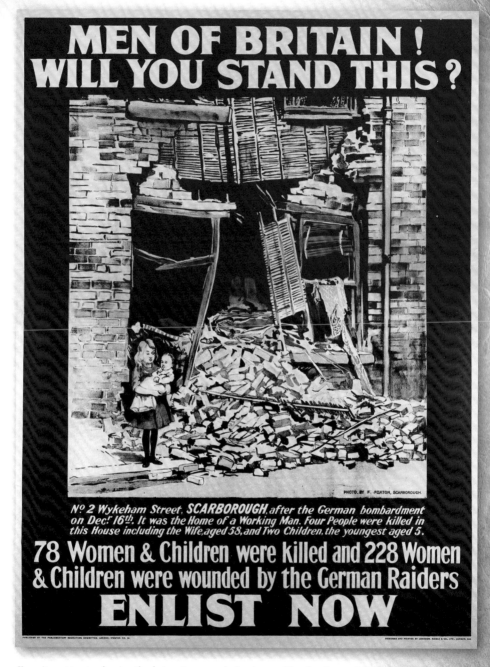

Recruitment poster showing the destruction wrought by the naval bombardment of Scarborough in December 1914. (MS 4383)

Birmingham City Battalions

On 28 August the *Birmingham Post* appealed to Birmingham men to enlist under the heading 'To Arms', and advocated raising a battalion that would be directly connected to the city. On the 29th, Alderman W.H. Bowater, the acting lord mayor, sent a telegram to the War Office offering to raise and equip a City of Birmingham Battalion, on the same principles as the 'pals' battalions already formed in Liverpool and Manchester. His offer was accepted. On the same day the *Post* carried an advertisement – 'A "City" Brigade. Who Will Join? An Appeal for Names' – which requested 1,000 men to come forward by the end of the week. The call was answered eagerly and the *Post* compiled a pre-recruitment list of volunteers which it published over the following days. By the evening of Saturday, 5 September, 4,500 names had been received. A special recruiting office was opened in the Art Gallery Extension and actual recruitment began on 7 September. The required number for the first battalion was reached within a week, and from 14 September enrolling began for a second battalion. Three City Battalions were recruited in total. Money was raised by public subscription from individuals, local firms and organisations to provide the three battalions with equipment. The men departed for their training, the first two City Battalions to Sutton Park and the third to Springfield College, Moseley, with an overflow of men billeted in local houses. Until their uniforms arrived they were dressed in civilian clothing, with a badge in their buttonhole to mark them out as City Battalion recruits. The 1st, 2nd and 3rd City Battalions were later officially known the 14th, 15th and 16th Service Battalions of the Royal Warwickshire Regiment.

Church Parade, Birmingham City Battalion in Corporation Street, 1915.
(MS 2724/2/B/3730)

Even when the army separation allowances were being paid, there were still cases where the family could not make ends meet and the Citizens' Committee became the local body responsible for the care and relief of dependants of soldiers and sailors. It could give supplementary grants for rent, sickness or in special emergencies. It could provide a maternity grant to poor mothers for four weeks before the birth and three weeks afterwards. It made grants to elderly parents who had lost the wages of one or more sons as well as to wives and children, and it could assist when soldiers returned home wounded. Widows were given help to fill official forms and correspond with official bodies, and the committee later also administered the War Pensions Act locally.[6] Like many charitable concerns, the committee's assistance went hand in hand with moral regulation of the behaviour of those in receipt of their help. The guide that they produced for their social workers indicates that they took a dim view of what they perceived as 'abuse of grants', particularly through 'drunkenness or shirking of work by husband in unemployment cases'. Unmarried mothers were also suspect and could not receive the army separation allowance, although the Citizens' Committee conceded that under certain circumstances it would consider making 'a grant from the Prince of Wales' Fund if a real home has been made for her'.[7]

In Birmingham, as elsewhere, the declaration of war prompted an outpouring of patriotic feelings and an initial rush to enlist in the colours. There were a considerable number of Army Reservists and Territorials in the city and it was these men who were affected first. The Reservists were mobilised immediately and included hundreds of men who worked for the city council's various departments and for local firms. Many of them had spent July at their annual training camp and in early August they were immediately drafted into the 1st and 2nd regular Battalions of the Royal Warwickshire Regiment. They were in France with the British Expeditionary Force before the month was out.[8]

On Sunday, 2 August, despite all the talk of oncoming war in the press, the Territorials departed for their annual training

Recruitment poster for the Warwickshire Volunteer Regiment, c. 1914–18. (MS 4383)

camp at Rhyl, accompanied by the city's lord mayor, Colonel E. Martineau, in his capacity as commanding officer of the 6th Battalion of the Royal Warwickshire Regiment. At 2 a.m. on 3 August, they received an order to return and headed back to Birmingham – the 5th and 6th Battalions to their drill hall in Thorp Street and 8th to their drill hall in Aston. The Territorials left Birmingham on the evening of 5 August for Weymouth, cheered on by a large crowd while Lord Mayor Martineau handed over his civic duties to his deputy, Alderman W.H. Bowater.

The local press reported proudly on the local response to the call to arms. By 7 August the *Birmingham Post* was writing of large crowds of young men outside the recruitment office in James Watt Street. The following day carried another report of the rush to join up in the city's recruitment office and concluded that it indicated 'a fine spirit of patriotism on the part of the young men of the city'.[9] Additional recruiting stations had to be opened at the Town Hall, where a large thermometer outside the building recorded the recruitment level in the city, and later in the Technical School in Suffolk Street, Curzon Hall and Queens' College. The Boy Scouts were pressed into action and 'Birmingham's Scout Army', as the *Weekly Mercury* put it, made itself useful in the Council House and at the recruitment depots.[10] A photograph on the back page of the *Birmingham Gazette* on 27 August showed a Scout holding up a placard emblazoned with the challenge 'I am too young to enlist. You are not.'[11]

In an oral history interview with staff from Birmingham Museum and Art Gallery in 1981, Victor Woolley recalled his reaction and that of three of his friends to the call to arms. At the time, Victor was an apprentice at Bucknam Webb's bookbinders in Church Street:

We there and then, the four of us, decided – although I was only 17½ – that we should join the forces. The four of us had been together all through school and, er, right up to the time of the war being declared and because they were older and decided to go I also decided to join them. The lord mayor of Birmingham appealed for a thousand boys to become the City of Birmingham Battalion but he got three thousand so three battalions were formed. Unfortunately two of my friends were in the Second City Battalion stationed at Powell's Pool and the Third City Battalion was stationed at Moseley College and I was one of those at Moseley. Erm, being under age, of course, I was a bit doubtful as to whether I should be allowed to stay and, hearing that the Second Battalion was starting a band, I applied and was transferred to the Second Battalion so I was with my other friends.[12]

He went on to describe his training in Sutton Park, recalling that at first they were in civilian clothes, with their membership of the City Battalions indicated by a lapel button of which he was 'very proud'. They were later issued with a blue uniform and a peak cap with the Royal Warwickshire Regiment badge.

The story of Harold W. Perry, an employee of Canning who enlisted as No. 465 in the 1st City Battalion and later reached the rank of captain, illustrates the considerations that faced men making the decision to join up. On 4 October 1914, the day before he departed to the training camp in Sutton, he wrote to his employer from his home at No. 38 Hall Road, Handsworth. His main concern was about an allowance of twenty-five shillings a week that the firm had promised to pay to his mother whilst he was away:

I have to pay 25/- into the house each week whether I am there or not & it is absolutely necessary that this amount be forthcoming – the more so now as my two brothers have enlisted & one of them (who is an engineer) will not be paying any money into the house at all during the time he is away. Briefly then it would not have been possible for me to have joined the Army if Mr Ernest [Canning] had not made it possible for me to do so by promising, through Mr Arthur, that 25/- would be paid to my mother during the time I was away. You will appreciate, I am sure, the sacrifice my mother is making in giving up three of her sons in answer to the Country's Call for men although, of course, she is proud to be able to do so but with regard to myself, as the eldest of the family, I consider that my first duty is to my mother.[13]

2nd City Battalion, leaving Sutton Coldfield for Yorkshire, June 1915. (MS 4616/2)

In June 1915, Harold moved with the rest of the City Battalions to a training camp in Yorkshire where they lived in tents. On 7 July 1915, he wrote from Wensley Camp, Leyburn, describing his experiences:

Training in Yorkshire, 1915. (MS 4616/2)

Since we have been here it has been brought home to us, rather forcibly, what a soldiers life is like & our quarters at Sutton were luxury in comparison. We rise at 5.30am & parade at 6.30 for Swedish drill, breakfast at 7.30 & parade again at 9 o/c [o'clock] for battalion or brigade operations. Battalion operations are usually over at 1 o/c but brigade operations last all through the day & we take our dinner with us (6oz meat & 2 potatoes & bread) & cook it ourselves. We had our first brigade field day yesterday starting out at 8 o/c am returning at 7.30 pm. The operations lasted until 5 o/c pm when we halted for dinner so that we went for 10 hours without food! A good many fellows found that they could not eat their dinner when they had cooked it, or rather tried to cook it, so had to remain hungry until they got back to Camp.[14]

He went on to say that they had covered 23 miles on the moors by the time they returned. Harold left for France with the rest of the battalion in November 1915 where, as we will see later, he was decorated for bravery.

GROWTH OF BIRMINGHAM
Birmingham's population grew rapidly during the nineteenth and twentieth centuries as the city industrialised. People moved to Birmingham to find work from other parts of Britain, Ireland and elsewhere in the world:

1801 –	73,670
1851 –	232,638
1901 –	522,204
1911 –	840,202
1921 –	919,444

Crossing to France, November 1915, photographed by J.A. Wall. (MS 4616/3)

The rise in patriotic feelings that stimulated men like Harold to enlist had unfortunate consequences for those residents of Birmingham who were 'enemy aliens'. At the time it was estimated that the number of Austrians and Germans in the city was between 700 and 800.[15] In the first few days of the war many were thrown out of work, and a few weeks later they lost their right to vote and men of military age were arrested and sent to internment camps. The local police arrested about twenty on 21 October, followed by another fifty the following day.[16] Many had British wives and families born in Birmingham who were left behind, often in dire need. Further arrests occurred in June 1915, when between fifty and sixty German men were sent from Birmingham to camps in Cheshire.[17]

Local Quakers were very concerned about the fate of the Germans and, by 11 August, J. Hotham Cadbury was co-ordinating offers of money and employment locally to relieve their plight. After they were interned he continued his efforts on their behalf, visiting the internment camps and organising collections of tools, books and games to be sent to the camps

in Handforth, Lancaster, Queensferry, Knockaloe and Douglas on the Isle of Man. The families of local internees also received support from the Quakers who provided Christmas presents for the children of forty-two families in December 1914.[18]

Unlike other parts of the country, Birmingham did not see anti-German riots until after the sinking of the ocean liner the *Lusitania* by German U-boats on 7 May 1915.[19] On the evening of Friday, 14 May, a disturbance broke out in John's Fish Restaurant at No. 45 High Street. The shop owner was Mrs Stackfeldt, who some years earlier had married John Stackfeldt. A crowd of about twenty came into the shop and threw objects around, eventually breaking a plate-glass window with a tin of sardines. The ringleaders were brought before the magistrates' court where the prosecuting solicitor maintained that the disturbance was the result 'of the present state of public feeling in consequence of the war' as it was believed that John was a German. As it turned out he was only 'technically' German, having been born in a part of Denmark that had been forcibly annexed by Germany and his parents were Danes. One of the accused said that he had 'suffered by the sinking of the *Lusitania*, and if I don't do it now I shall do it some other time'. The magistrate retaliated that the proper way of showing their patriotism would be to enlist, 'and he could not understand why three strong-looking men like the prisoners had not shown their patriotism in that way'.[20]

The outbreak of war resulted in a marked increase in the regulation of various aspects of life on the home front – by the government, the local authorities, and by the voluntary sector. By the autumn of 1914, concerns were growing among the civic elite that disruption to family life and the usual order was leading to a collapse of public morality and to unacceptable behaviour, particularly by women. The wives of soldiers who were absent at the front were the subject of a moral panic that fed newspaper columns across the country. On 23 October 1914, the *Birmingham Post* published an article

> The Aliens Restriction Act 1914 was rushed through Parliament on 5 August to control 'enemy aliens' in the UK. Such persons had to register with the police, where they could live was restricted, and they could be deported. During the war about 32,000 'aliens' were arrested and interned across the UK.

investigating allegations that women whose husbands were away in the forces, and who were in receipt of the government separation allowance, were spending their time and money in the pub. The situation was, the *Post* railed, 'depraving to the women, bad, unutterably bad, in its effects upon their children and home life generally, disloyal to men risking their lives at the call of their country'.[21] There was also a concern about so-called 'Khaki fever' and the effect that large numbers of soldiers training in the neighbourhood might have on the behaviour and morals of young working-class women.

Although the leadership of Birmingham's women's organisations considered the reports to be greatly exaggerated, they were also concerned. They initiated measures to regulate and police the situation, and to provide alternative 'safe' entertainment for working-class women. The local branch of the National Union of Women Workers successfully campaigned for a reduction in the opening hours of public houses. The National Union was not a trade union as the name might suggest but an organisation of middle-class women. They petitioned the chief constable and the chairman of the Licensing Justices Committee and mobilised another 100 societies in Birmingham to do the same for the sake of 'the welfare of Birmingham – indeed … the welfare of the British Empire'.[22]

To regulate the behaviour of women in public places they established a Women's Patrol Committee to co-ordinate a volunteer force of over thirty-five women to walk the streets, ensuring that working-class women were behaving themselves. These women were middle class and often had a background in charitable social work or teaching and received 'instruction in police control and in methods of girl life'. They were not uniformed, but wore plain clothing with an armband and carried a card of authority from the chief constable. They patrolled regular

Birmingham's wartime lord and lady mayoress played a very active role in organising and directing aspects of the city's home front:

AUGUST–SEPTEMBER 1914
Colonel and Mrs Ernest Martineau

SEPTEMBER 1914–NOVEMBER 1915
W.H. and Mrs Bowater

NOVEMBER 1915–DECEMBER 1916
Neville and Mrs Chamberlain

JANUARY 1917–SEPTEMBER 1919
David and Mrs Brooks

beats in the Thorp Street area, in Moseley, Harborne and Great Brook Street, and in Witton. From the beginning, the Patrols Committee realised that there was little point in clearing young women off the streets if they had nowhere else to go, and the emphasis was therefore on providing counter attractions through various clubs and activities. A 'Patriotic Club for Girls' was opened at 'cheerful premises' in No. 137a Suffolk Street which recruited a membership of 166 girls in the first month, and 'Ladywood Parlour', a club for the wives of soldiers and sailors, opened at No. 118 Ledsam Parade at a subscription of two pence per week, with an attached nursery provided for infants.[23]

Newspaper photograph of Mrs Rebecca Lipscombe and Mrs Evelyn Myles, Birmingham's first female police officers (Birmingham Weekly Mercury, 9 June 1917)

Once the voluntary patrols were established, the National Union began pressing for official women police officers. The Watch Committee, which was responsible for the police force, initially refused to appoint women, a bitter disappointment to the campaigners who pointed to initiatives in Southampton, Hull, Liverpool and Huddersfield.[24] The National Union, the Women's Labour League and the Women's Co-operative Guild continued campaigning throughout 1915 and 1916 and finally, on 14 May 1917, the Watch Committee recommended the appointment of two female police officers, Mrs Rebecca Lipscombe and Mrs Evelyn Myles, who were already employed as 'matrons in the Central Lock-up'.[25] They were paid thirty-five shillings per week with uniform, but did not have powers of arrest and were limited to specific duties with women and children for which, as women, they were deemed to have a natural affinity. Two further women, Mrs Elsie Chapman and Mrs Divelly, were appointed in September and October.[26]

The war also had a marked effect on what the city felt and looked like, and one of the most noticeable early changes was in the regulation of lights. As a large industrial city, Birmingham was felt to be a natural target for enemy air raids and civil defence measures were brought in to reduce the risk. As early as 23 November 1914, the city's chief constable, Charles Haughton Rafter, issued a notice under the provisions of the Defence of the Realm Act for the reduction of lights in the city, a move that at the time was criticised as overzealous and creating an unnecessarily depressing effect. Preparations were also made from January 1915 for the sounding of an audible alarm in the event of an attack. In fact it was another year before Zeppelins were seen in the locality. At about 8 p.m. on 31 January 1916, explosions were heard in the distance in the north of Birmingham as German Zeppelins struck at the Black Country, where several people were killed and many injured. Although Birmingham itself

Lady Mayoress Martineau launched HMS *Birmingham* on 7 May 1913. On 9 August 1914, HMS *Birmingham* sank German U-boat U-15, the first of the war. She took part in the Battle of Heligoland in August, the Battle of Dogger Bank in 1915, and the Battle of Jutland in 1916.

POLICE NOTICE.

AIRCRAFT RAIDS.

DEFENCE OF THE REALM REGULATIONS.

By direction of the competent Military Authority the FOLLOWING PRECAUTIONS WILL BE TAKEN FOR THE PUBLIC SAFETY IN CASE OF ATTACK BY ENEMY AIRCRAFT.

In order to avoid the possibility of misunderstanding the only authority authorised to give instructions for sounding an alarm in Birmingham on the reported approach of enemy aircraft will be the Chief Constable, who has made arrangements with certain firms to sound, when notified by him, their steam bulls and hooters. No firms except those who have been arranged with will take part in sounding the alarm.

THIS ALARM WILL CONSIST OF FIVE NOTES, THE LAST NOTE BEING MORE PROLONGED THAN THE OTHERS; in the manner adopted by railwaymen in case of accident. It is called by them "the Cock Crow." IT WILL BE REPEATED FOR ABOUT FIVE MINUTES.

All Persons are warned that in case of an alarm being sounded as described, or a bomb being dropped from aircraft, or if they hear the sound of anti-aircraft guns being fired, that the cellars are the refuges which offer the best chance of safety.

All Persons are warned of the extreme danger of being in the streets when anti-aircraft guns are being fired, as the shrapnel bullets scatter in all directions over wide areas, rendering the streets very dangerous.

On an alarm being sounded by steam bulls and hooters all outside lights of every description will be extinguished at once, and kept extinguished for the rest of the night.

Factories which are at work during the night should also on such alarm extinguish their lights.

At night the most important precaution is to show no lights which would be visible from aircraft and enable them to identify the towns or other places on which they propose to drop bombs.

The public will please note that the object of the scheme set forth above is purely precautionary, and that no unnecessary apprehension of danger need be caused by its publication.

PERSONS CAUSING FALSE ALARMS TO BE SOUNDED ARE LIABLE TO SEVERE PENALTIES under the Defence of the Realm Act and Regulations.

CHARLES HAUGHTON RAFTER,

27th January, 1915.   **CHIEF CONSTABLE.**

(9230)   PERCIVAL JONES LIMITED, 148-149, GREAT CHARLES STREET, BIRMINGHAM.

*Police notice of air-raid precautions, 27 January 1915. (*Birmingham Scrapbook *vol. 7)*

was not attacked, public transport in the city came to a standstill. Despite being warned of the 'extreme danger' of being on the streets during an attack, the excitement brought many people out of doors. Elizabeth Cadbury was at a meeting of the adult school at Severn Street and wrote of her surprise at leaving the meeting at about 9.30 p.m. 'to find the city plunged in darkness, all the trams stopped, crowds of people in the streets, and to hear that Zeppelins were in the neighbourhood, probably at Dudley'. As the police refused to let her driver move the car she and her daughter Dollie walked to Priory Road, where she reported seeing 'crowds of people standing along the street; the works in the neighbourhood having all stopped and the traffic, there was none of the usual vibration and noise – a very curious effect'. She was finally given permission to use the car as long as they travelled without lights, and they had 'a perilous journey home in the dark … nearly annihilated by a huge motor waggon, also without lights, coming towards us on the wrong side of the road'.[27]

Following the raid the lord mayor, Neville Chamberlain, and other civic leaders in the Midlands, instigated a review and petitioned London for better precautions and anti-aircraft measures. Zeppelins did not return to Birmingham until the following year, on 19 October 1917, when the noise of the engines was clearly heard and many people saw the danger overhead. The Zeppelin passed over the city, which was in darkness with the exception of the Austin Works, which were brilliantly lit. Consequently, a bomb hit one of the outlying buildings, injuring two people. After this, raid precautions in the form of telephone warning systems, aerial searchlights and anti-aircraft guns were again improved. The last Zeppelin attack occurred on 12 April 1918 when five airships attacked the Midlands. One of the airships came near Birmingham at about 11.30 p.m. but was driven off by anti-aircraft fire. Two bombs were dropped by the airship as it flew over the city, one on the Robin Hood Golf Course and the other on Manor Farm, but no one was injured.

Endnotes

1   *Birmingham Post*, 2 August 1914, p. 3.
2   *Birmingham Post*, 5 August 1914, p. 3; 6 August, p. 3.
3   MS 1410/5/1.
4   MS 517/A/8/1/4.
5   S56/2/2.
6   E.M.R. Shakespear, 'Birmingham Citizens' Committee', *Women Workers*, March 1917, pp. 97–105.
7   *Guide for Helpers*, 1914, L41.2/254291.
8   For details of the movement of the Reservists, Territorials and for a detailed account of the involvement of the City Battalions in the war see Terry Carter, *Birmingham Pals: A History of the Three City Battalions Raised in Birmingham in the Great War* (Barnsley: The Pen and Sword Books, 2011).
9   *Birmingham Post*, 7 August 1914, p. 3; 8 August, p. 8.
10 *Birmingham Weekly Mercury*, 29 August 1914, p. 1.
11 *Birmingham Gazette*, 27 August 1914, p. 6.
12 R0089 Victor Woolley © Birmingham Museums Trust.
13 MS 2326/1/9/1.
14 MS 2326/1/9/3.
15 *The Manchester Guardian*, 23 October 1914, p. 6.
16 *The Manchester Guardian*, 25 September 1914, p. 2; *Birmingham Post*, 23 October 1914, p. 8.
17 *The Manchester Guardian*, 28 June 1915, p. 5.
18 Warwickshire North Monthly Meeting, 11 August 1914; 12 January 1915; 16 March 1915.
19 *The Manchester Guardian*, 14 May 1915, p. 3.
20 *Birmingham Post*, 17 May 1915, p. 3.
21 *Birmingham Post,* 23 October 1914, p. 4.
22 *Women Workers*, December 1914, p. 81.
23 *Women Workers*, March 1915, pp. 96–99, 108; June 1915, pp. 16–20.
24 Minutes, BCC 1/AC/3/1/10; *Women Workers*, June 1915, p. 20.
25 Minutes, BCC 1/AC/1/1/24.
26 Minutes, BCC 1/AC/1/1/24.
27 MS 466/1/1/15/3/13.

2

EXILE AND REFUGE

War brought new communities of people to the city. From the beginning of the war the press was full of dreadful stories of German war atrocities in Belgium and as early as 1 September plans were afoot to help Belgian refugees. The Birmingham War Refugees Committee was established under the chairmanship of Elizabeth Cadbury and included members from various religious and political organisations across the city. Local Quakers like the Cadbury family were particularly active. Within days No. 44 Islington Row was provided as a headquarters and hostel and donations of furniture, clothing and accommodation began to arrive. Barrow and Geraldine Cadbury offered Uffculme and Walter Chamberlain donated Harborne Hall. The first party of fifty refugees arrived on Friday, 4 September, and Elizabeth wrote that there was 'tremendous excitement in New Street, as word got round that the first Belgians were arriving, and they finally departed to Uffculme in a char-a-banc amidst great cheers'.[1]

For the first few weeks the War Refugees Committee was incredibly busy as groups arrived regularly, sometimes before the previous arrivals had been processed and accommodated. One week in October 1914 provides a snapshot of the situation. On Monday, 12 October, a telegram arrived from London asking the committee to take 500 Belgians. Barrow and Geraldine Cadbury responded by providing Moseley Road Institute and by Thursday it was equipped for 400 people. At 8.40 p.m. on Wednesday 300 arrived at New Street Station and had to be processed and allocated. At 1.50 p.m. on Thursday another 100 arrived, followed by a further 240 on Friday afternoon. The following Monday Elizabeth Cadbury wrote that 'from 9 o'clock in the morning until 7 o'clock at night did we wrestle with the huge number of people at Moseley Road'.[2] During its first year the Birmingham War Refugees Committee dealt with over 5,000 Belgian refugees.[3]

In addition to housing the refugees, the committee and its volunteers distributed gifts of clothing, boots and other items, they organised English lessons, and on 26 October 1914 a Lost Relatives Bureau was established. An employment committee found work, particularly for the men. A Belgian Club, 'Le Cercle Belge', was opened in No. 81 Islington Row for the use of male refugees. It was open from 2–9 every weekday, and women and children

The children of the 'Ecole Belge', or Birmingham's Belgian school, 1918. (LF21.86/531707)

Ecole Belge, Birmingham, 1918.

were admitted on Sundays when it was 'always thronged'. Coffee and cakes were supplied and books, games and a gramophone were provided. The first refugee placed in charge of the club was a cafe proprietor from Brussels but he resigned when the committee refused to buy a barrel of beer.[4]

The Birmingham War Refugees Committee also ran a maternity home under the direction of Geraldine Southall Cadbury at No. 19 Carpenter Road in Edgbaston, where fifty-eight Belgian children were born by August 1916. Initially Belgian children attended local schools but, by October 1915, demand was growing for a specifically Belgian education so that the children would find it easier to adjust when they returned home. The Belgian school finally opened on 14 February 1916 to educate the children 'on national lines and in their national languages'. It had Belgian teachers and was supported financially by the Belgian Government. By 15 March 1916 it had eighty-one pupils, which increased to 124 by October 1916. They were taught in French and Flemish, and religious teaching was provided by a Belgian Catholic priest, Father Maeysmans.[5]

As is so often the case with the history of refugees, the archive is silent when it comes to the refugees' own voices and opinions, and we are left with nothing more than a list of names in a register. Occasionally, however, we get a rare glimpse of the individuals and the stories behind the names. August De Haes, a 32-year-old tailor and his 28-year-old wife Dymphna, came originally from Lierre near Malines. They arrived in Birmingham on 20 January 1915 with their three children, Elisa (age 9), Frans (age 2) and baby Lodewyck, and lived for a time at No. 60 Ashmore Road. Sadness struck the family a few weeks later when Lodewyck died. His death was registered by Kings Norton Registrar when his name was given as Luduriscus. Another child, Joanes, was born to the couple on 16 August, and it is impossible to tell which of the two boys is seen sitting on his mother's knee in the photograph. August's parents, Frans and Melanie,

The First World War created millions of refugees. In addition to the Belgians, a third of Serbia's pre-war population had to flee their homes following the country's defeat. Armenians fled before the massacres by Turkish troops, and there were an estimated 6 million refugees in the Russian Empire.

The De Haes family, 1915. (MS 466/51/39)

and his two sisters, Victoria (age 21) and Maria (age 17), also came to Birmingham where they came under the care of the forewomen at Cadburys, and the two sisters were employed by the firm.[6]

The numbers of refugees arriving slowed down considerably after the first year of the war but most remained in Birmingham until early 1919 when a farewell event was held at the Town Hall on 6 January. Elizabeth Cadbury and Geraldine Southall Cadbury were both awarded the medal of Queen Elizabeth of the Belgians in recognition of their work on behalf of the refugees.

The Belgians were not the only refugees to find a home in the city. In early 1916, a hostel for twenty-five Serbian boys, aged 10 to 14, was opened at The Elms in Selly Oak. They were part of a group of 300 who had been brought to the UK by the Serbian Relief Fund. The hostel was rechristened 'Serbia House' and administered by local Quakers – Elizabeth Cadbury chaired the committee, W.A. Albright was treasurer, J. Douglas Maynard and his wife looked after the boys, and Alan Geale was their scoutmaster. When the boys arrived on Saturday, 20 May with their Serbian schoolmaster, they were met by a band of Birmingham Boy Scouts and 'marched up to the house with flags flying'.[7]

Wounded servicemen also arrived in Birmingham from all over the world. In addition to the British armed forces, local hospitals treated soldiers from Belgium, Australia, Canada, New Zealand, America and Italy. Plans for receiving the wounded were in hand long before the war began. The 1st Southern General Hospital had been founded in 1908 as a Territorial General Hospital and Birmingham University was therefore prepared to be used in the event of war.[8] The order to mobilise was received at 7.45 p.m. on 4 August, and the following day the Royal Army Medical Corps Territorial Unit made its way from its Great Brook Street headquarters to the university, where beds and mattresses were already beginning to arrive. The first convoy of 120 sick and wounded was received on 1 September, and by the end of the year there had been twenty-one convoys. By the end of 1914, the 1st Southern General had expanded to 800 beds and 3,892 patients had been received. Soldiers who died at the hospital were buried at Lodge Hill Cemetery.[9]

Wounded servicemen were brought to Birmingham by ambulance train, and on the first occasion it took four and a half hours to unload all the patients. From late September 1914, the

goods station at Selly Oak was used to receive patients destined for the hospital. A rest station was established for soldiers and sailors at Snow Hill early in the war and members of the local Voluntary Aid Detachment (VAD) provided refreshments of tea, cake, fruit, sweets and cigarettes for the wounded on ambulance trains passing through Birmingham, with jelly and sponge cake for the most seriously wounded. Postcards and pencils were also given out. The rest station provided for some 362,000 men on 2,372 trains during the war and finally closed its doors at the end of May 1919, when it was no longer considered necessary. A similar rest station was provided at New Street Station run by a voluntary committee. In the first two years, transport from the train stations to the hospitals was often undertaken by volunteers – who used their own cars and paid for their own petrol until a Voluntary Aid Detachment Motor Transport was established in 1916. E.M. Tailby designed a trailer-ambulance that could be attached to ordinary cars

Nurses and patients in ward B1 of the 1st Southern General Hospital, formerly the Mechanical Engineering Department of the University of Birmingham, 1914. (MS 2724/2/B/3518)

to carry two stretcher cases. His design was approved by the medical authorities and twenty-five of these trailers were in use in Birmingham during the war.

As the numbers of wounded men increased, further capacity was needed and the 1st Southern General opened a number of auxiliary hospitals including Dudley Road Infirmary, which opened as a section of the 1st Southern General in May 1915. The first convoy arrived at Dudley Road on 10 May 1915 and the hospital used the goods station at Soho and Winson Green to unload patients. It became a separate war hospital in its own right from 1917, and over the course of the war 53,896 patients were treated there in addition to outpatients. Extra capacity was also provided by two schools in Selly Park and Kings Heath that were taken over to provide another two auxiliary hospitals of 225 beds, each supplemented by tents, that opened in October 1915.[10] The Monyhull Section of the 1st Southern General opened on 23 November 1916 with 400 beds.

Local mental hospitals were also turned over to the war effort. Rubery Hill, later known as 1st Birmingham War Hospital, opened on 30 July 1915, and Hollymoor, later the 2nd Birmingham War Hospital, on 5 July. By 31 March 1919, Rubery had treated 20,015 patients, and Hollymoor 16,780. From the end of 1917 Hollymoor was converted into an orthopaedic hospital with massage and electrical departments, a gymnasium, curative baths and workshop facilities, staffed initially by American specialists. The workshops made equipment such as splints and bed frames used in the wards, and an education officer organised lectures and classes in a range of subjects including French, Spanish, commercial arithmetic, shorthand, bookkeeping and gardening.

Still more beds were needed, however, and several large private houses were lent or donated by their owners. These included, among others, Moor Green Hall in Moseley from November 1914, Lordswood in Harborne and The Norlands in Erdington from May 1915, The Beeches in Bournville from December 1915, Stoneleigh in Stechford from July 1916, and Farcroft in Handsworth from June 1917. Uffculme, which had earlier been used to house refugees, was converted into a hospital run by the Friends Ambulance Unit from November 1916.

Highbury, the former residence of Joseph Chamberlain, opened as a Voluntary Aid Detachment Hospital with 140 beds on 28 May 1915. The equipment and fittings were paid for by the employees of Kynoch Works. The hospital used all the available space including the conservatories and the greenhouses, and Barry Jackson of the Birmingham Repertory Theatre paid for an extension block in the grounds. Highbury provided electrical and massage treatments, gymnastics, and gradually added more neurological beds. Curative workshops were provided in carpentry, tailoring, gardening, cooking, boot and shoe repairs, and making splints. The hospital was staffed by a matron, eight nursing sisters and twenty-six VAD nurses and support staff.

Ethel Violet Jackson recalled her days as a VAD at Highbury in an oral history interview with Birmingham Museum and Art Gallery staff in 1986. Ethel was born in 1897. She was the daughter of George Jackson, a well-to-do wholesale fruit

Wounded soldiers convalescing at Highbury Hospital. (MS 4616/17)

39

Voluntary Aid Detachments were first created in 1909. They were volunteers and came mostly from the middle or upper classes. Often trained by the St John's Ambulance, VAD nurses served in hospitals in Britain and cared for the wounded alongside military nurses in France, Gallipoli, Mesopotamia and elsewhere.

merchant, and during the war the family lived at The Firs in Elvetham Road, Edgbaston.[11] To begin with her father was reluctant to give his permission for her to volunteer as he was worried about her meeting soldiers and hearing 'rough' language, an unfounded fear as Ethel later recalled that the wounded soldiers were always very respectful. Eventually her father agreed and paid for her uniform. She arrived at Highbury in February 1918 at the age of 21 after training at St John's Ambulance classes on the Bristol Road. She recalled a very organised institution where she and her colleagues addressed each other by their surnames. Ethel described the tensions between the regular nurses and the VAD volunteers, a frequent occurrence in hospitals both at home and at the front. When Ethel was asked to take charge of the plaster room she was approached by the hospital's matron who said:

The gymnasium at Highbury Hospital. (MS 4616/17)

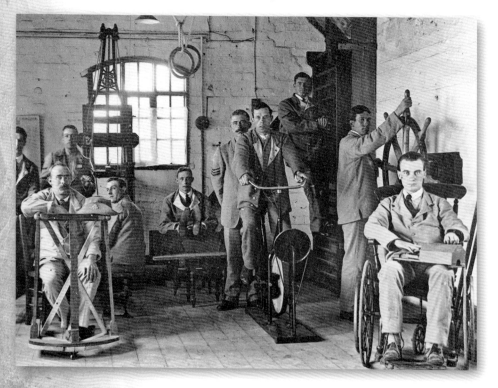

VAD nurses and staff at Highbury Hospital with Commandant Mrs Porter sitting in the centre, 1917–18. (MS 4616/17)

'You have caused some trouble!' So I said, 'What have I done?' She said, 'There's been a meeting of all the Sisters. They're all furious that a nurse should have been put in charge of a department.'

Volunteering at Highbury changed Ethel's life. In 1919 she married the pioneering orthopaedic surgeon Naughton Dunn whom she met at Highbury. Dunn had been associated with the 'Birmingham Royal Cripples', the forerunner of the Royal Orthopaedic Hospital, since 1913 and served as a major in the Royal Army Medical Corps during the war. He operated on patients at Highbury and other hospitals in the area. Together with Sir Robert Jones, with whom he had trained in Liverpool, Dunn developed new ways of treating wounded servicemen.

A humorous insight into life at Highbury was preserved in a personal album kept by a former VAD, presumably composed by a nurse or patient:

TEN LITTLE V.A.DS. (1916)

TEN little V.A.Ds. at dinner in a line,
One dropped four plates at once and then there were nine.
NINE little V.A.Ds. came on duty late,
The Matron interviewed one, and then there were eight.
EIGHT little V.A.Ds. with passes till eleven,
One returned at 2 a.m. and then there were seven.
SEVEN little V.A.Ds. with batt'ries playing tricks
One got an electric shock, and then there were six.
SIX little V.A.Ds. very much alive,
One overworked herself and then there were five.
FIVE little V.A.Ds. put Ronuk on the floor,
One came a cropper there, and then there were four.
FOUR little V.A.Ds. getting patients tea,
The bread machine cut up one and then there were three.
THREE little V.A.Ds. doesn't matter who,
One cheeked the Commandant, and then there were two.
TWO little V.A.Ds. thought their work was done,
One forgot the locker tops, and then there was one.
ONE little V.A.D. thought it time to run,
A Zeppelin fell on Highbury, and then there were none.[12]

Considerable efforts were devoted to providing entertainment and alleviating the boredom of the wounded men in all the local hospitals. At the 1st Southern General the Rowland Mason Memorial Hut was provided in August 1917 equipped with a stage and dressing rooms, and about 500 full shows were held there for audiences of over 200,000 men. Amateur and professional companies performed for the patients at all the hospitals, and activities such as games, lectures and film shows were organised. The patients of the 1st Southern General had their own hospital magazine *The Southern Cross* and Highbury had its own concert party. As well as home-grown entertainment, venues in the city including the Theatre Royal, the Alexandra, the Prince of Wales Theatre, the Gaiety and the Hippodrome provided seats for the wounded.

Christmas entertainment at Highbury Hospital. (MS 4616/17)

Birmingham VADs also served abroad. Marion J. Cadbury, daughter of Elizabeth and George Cadbury and known as Mollie, left England on 16 April 1915 bound for the St Pierre Friends Ambulance Unit Hospital in Dunkirk. Mollie sent regular letters home which reflect both quiet times, when she and her friend Olga M. Wilson went bicycling round the countryside and even played a little hockey, and stressful periods dealing with casualties. Like most nurses, Mollie was keen to serve near the front line. On 26 April 1915, she wrote from Dunkirk that 'The Germans seem to be having a good try this time any way, and I am jolly glad I'm out here, though I don't expect I'll be lucky enough to get any of the excitement.' A few weeks later, on 11 May, things were hotting up:

As I expect you will already have heard by the time this letter has made its lengthy progress to you, we have been having some more free exhibitions of fireworks. There are seemingly two lines of fire, one over the ------ ----- [censored] hospital, and one about a quarter of a mile inland, aiming respectively at the --------- sheds and town and clocks, it is therefore only when the shells fall short that we get them near us … Everyone says that at present St. Pierre is quite safe, as it is about 300 yards to the right of the line of fire. When the shells fall short the noise is pretty ear-splitting, and the whole place shakes and rattles. We are always very glad to find our digs safe when we return at night, as they are opposite the Kursaal and might receive a stray shot!

During summer 1915 Mollie transferred to No. 3 British Red Cross Hospital at Abbeville. On 26 July she explained to her parents: 'We get the worst cases here, as it is the first place where the wounded stop to get their wounds dressed, and only those are taken out who cannot travel farther.' Like all nurses in base hospitals near the front she saw the horror of war at first hand. On 'about' 11 September she wrote:

I come off night duty in a week's time, and shall be jolly glad in many ways, as one does long for a good night's sleep. We had some very bad cases in yesterday, one man with his face burnt away with liquid fire; there is very little left & most of his jaw and mouth being gone, one pushes a tube down his throat for food. He is a fine, tall and muscular man, and it is simply fearful to see him. I think liquid fire and bullets with liquid fire are by far the most diabolical things yet invented, and that is saying a lot.[13]

It wasn't all grim, however, and Mollie met her future husband, Bill Greeves, in France where he served alongside her brother Laurence in the Friends Ambulance Unit. They were married in Bournville in February 1918.

Not all women could volunteer as nurses and a range of women's groups and organisations supported the war effort in different ways. New organisations, such as the Women's Voluntary Reserve and the League of Honour for Women and Girls of the British Empire, were formed for the duration. Aimed at women and girls over the age of 14, the League of Honour had a strong moral emphasis and focused on 'upholding the standard of women's duty and honour' by combatting 'some of the social and moral dangers emphasised by the war'.[14] An inaugural meeting was held at the Town Hall on the evening of Monday, 14 December 1914 where the attendance was so large that an overflow meeting for about 300 had to be accommodated at Queen's College and many women and girls went away disappointed at not being able to get in. By June 1915 it was reported that there were almost 10,000 members in Birmingham, and a Junior League was organised in schools for girls between the ages of 12 and 14.[15] Members engaged in sewing, making parcels for soldiers and the wounded, and collecting money for the Star and Garter Home for Disabled Soldiers at Richmond.[16] Their motto was 'Strength and Honour' and every member swore to 'uphold the Honour of Our Empire and its Defenders in this time of War, by Prayer, Purity, and Temperance'.[17]

The Lady Mayoress' Depot was established soon after the outbreak of war. Its initial purpose was to supply clothing for soldiers and co-ordinate the voluntary efforts of the many sewing parties that were founded by women in over 200 centres across the city. The depot supplied shirts, cardigans, gloves, socks, belts, mufflers, mittens and blankets, and during the first four months 40,146 articles of clothing were sent to men serving in the forces, concentrating initially on battalions particularly connected with Birmingham. They also sent chocolate, cigarettes, games, musical instruments and gramophones, often donated by the employees of local firms or council departments.

Parcels sent to Birmingham prisoners of war by the Lady Mayoress' Depot:

1914–April 1917 – 39,873
April–December 1917 – 31,165
January–November 1918 – 59,124

130,162 parcels were sent in total. The depot issued 273,533 garments to servicemen, and collected 24,536 items of clothing for distressed local civilians.

BIRMINGHAM WOMEN'S VOLUNTARY RESERVE

The Women's Voluntary Reserve (WVR) was a national patriotic organisation founded in August 1914 by Evelina Haverfield. Mrs R.C. Hopkins approached Birmingham's lady mayoress and suggested forming a local battalion. The initial meeting on 22 January 1915 recruited 700 volunteers, which increased to 1,200 by March. They completed a form providing information about their proficiency in riding, driving, cycling, running, signalling and shooting. A fee of one shilling was paid on 'enlistment', they were medically examined, and discipline, *esprit de corps* and physical fitness were emphasised. The uniform consisted of a khaki Norfolk coat, skirt, shirt and tie, brown shoes, spat puttees and a felt hat; officers also wore a leather belt and dogskin gloves. Mrs Hopkins became the battalion's colonel.

The WVR was controversial due to its perceived military nature – the uniform, use of military rank, strict discipline, and activities such as drill and marching all gave the impression that they were stepping beyond what was considered acceptable behaviour for women. The local branch was at pains to stress that although 'People have feared that women wished to become soldiers' it was a '*non*-political and *non*-military organisation'. Headquarters was at No. 3 New Street, with branches at Harborne, King's Norton, Selly Oak, Handsworth, Erdington, Moseley, and Sutton Coldfield. The recruits were formed into companies, and undertook training in Swedish drill, French, signalling, First Aid, home nursing and cooking. They organised lodgings for munition workers, canteens and street collections, and they assisted with the transport of the wounded to local war hospitals. They provided guards of honour at public events, and undertook the security at Birmingham Museum and Art Gallery, enabling it to stay open despite the depletion of its staff. From 1916 they also assisted with agricultural work on the land.

Colonel Hopkins of Birmingham Women's Voluntary Reserve in uniform. (MS 3194/1)

From 1915 the depot provided war hospitals at home and abroad with items such as swabs, bandages and pneumonia jackets, and local branches were formed in Streetly, Erdington, Stourbridge and Acock's Green. Between March 1916 and February 1919, 1,100 workers made 827,176 articles, and provided 8,000 articles a month for two base hospitals in France alone. In November 1916, a carpentry branch was established in Edgbaston by Walter Dobson, later run by his brother H.A. Dobson, which made stools, bed tables and over 600 crutches for wounded soldiers. From July 1916 the depot also organised entertainment and occupation for soldiers who were wounded or convalescing in local hospitals, and they took on responsibility for overseeing the graves of Colonial soldiers who died locally.

From late 1914 one of the depot's most important functions was its parcel service for Birmingham prisoners of war, to whom it sent clothing, comforts and food. The parcels were made up by volunteers under the supervision of Mrs Jespers, the superintendent. By the middle of June 1915 the depot had a list of 632 individual prisoners and they aimed to send one parcel to each man every fortnight at a cost of three shillings each. Money was raised through fundraising events, such as a special matinee performance by Miss Mary Anderson at the Theatre Royal

Window display in the Lady Mayoress' Depot showing sample parcels, c. 1917. (LF75.7/ 530991)

Volunteers making up parcels for prisoners of war, c. 1917. (LF75.7/530991)

on 23 October 1918 which raised £5,389. Relatives and other subscribers could 'adopt' a POW, and employees of firms often adopted former workmates. Contact details were given to the subscriber so that they could also write to the man. By May 1916 the depot was supplying 850 men in Germany, Austro-Hungary and Turkey with parcels, 542 of whom had been adopted by individuals or groups.

That the service was much appreciated by the POWs is obvious from the many postcards and letters of thanks received by the depot. The correspondence also clearly demonstrates that the contact with home, and the thought that someone cared, was as important as the food in the parcel. For some men it was their only remaining connection with the outside world. In September 1918, Private J. Hackett, of the 15th Battalion, Royal Warwickshire Regiment, wrote from Stammlager, Friederichfeld, Germany. He had been taken prisoner on 26 October 1917 and had received regular parcels for the first few months. However, he was now very worried by the lack of contact with home:

Prisoner's Acknowledgment.

Name Pte, J, T, Hackett   33207

Address 15 Batt Royal Warwickshire Regt, Stammlager, Friederichfeld Deutschland E, K, 6

Dear Madam and all included in your society many thanks for your food parcel received 27/6/18 which was in excellent condition there was no number on it. & remain yours thankfully
Pte J T Hackett
50 Allesly Street
B,ham,

3 MAY

Thank you postcard sent to the Lady Mayoress' Depot from J. Hackett, 1918. (LF75.7/530991)

... since April the 20th I have not received a line from anyone in England whatever and now it is the 11th of September. The last letter I had was to say my mother had just been very ill, so you may be able to tell that I am beggining [sic] to worry. This is my home address Mr J. Hackett 50 Allesley Street, Birmingham, England, trusting you will find everything in very good condition, as I for myself am very well considering, I must thank you for your food parcels they are very nice indeed and they come here in very good condition.[18]

The letters received by the Lady Mayoress' Depot also give an insight into the conditions under which some of the men were living, and are touchingly grateful and apologetic for 'troubling' the committee, or being a burden to those at home. Corporal H. Simpson, of the 9th *Royal Warwickshires* wrote from a camp near Constantinople, Turkey, on 17 February 1918:

... i [sic] am sorry to say that we are having very severe weather here every day snow and frost and we cannot buy tea or sugar at any price and it would be a God send to get a good Drink of Tea i am very sorry to put you to the trouble as it is needed very badly out here i am sorry to say that i got sent to this place owing to my ill health, Kind Friend i hope you will excuse my impertinance for being so forward but under the circumstances i am compeled to ask you, as i am a native of B,ham, i thought you was the only person i could appeal to, i hope and trust you will kindly acknowldege my letter and let me know if you can oblige as i hope this will not put you or your committee to any inconvenience.

Corporal C. Batcheltor, 2/8 *Royal Warwickshire Regiment* wrote from Scheveningen, The Hague in Holland, on 21 June 1918 describing the conditions under which he and his fellow prisoners had survived:

On board the HMS Marlborough, a photograph sent to the Lady Mayoress' Depot from prisoners of war, c. 1916. A 'knut' was a slang term for a fashionable or showy young man. (LF75.7/530991)

As you have probably heard the german [*sic*] food was awful, our daily rations consisted of the following, (Breakfast,) a substitute for coffee, which was like drinking poison itself, for this meal we had nothing to eat just the coffee to drink, (dinner). For this meal we would get soup made from mangel wurzels, and each man had a small basin, (for tea) we had more soup, which the fellows nicknamed water soup and we also received a small piece of bread, which would not weigh 4 ozs. And I have seen the bread when it has been green with mould … and I have seen the fellows collapse through hunger and weakness, for at that time it was too soon to have parcels come from England, and so we had to live on German rations. and [*sic*] I honestly think that but for the goodness of you and thousands more, that there is many fellows who would not be alive today, I think they would have died of starvation.[19]

Private David William Harwood of the 2/2 South Midland Field Ambulance, Royal Army Medical Corps, was a prisoner of war in Flavey-le-Martel from March 1918. After the war he was a tram driver living in Benson Road and in May 1921 travelled to Leipzig

*Watercolour of
Ruhleben internment
camp by William
Powell, 1918.*
(MS 3767)

to give evidence in the war trial of a Captain Emil Muller who was on trial for ill-treating the prisoners under his command. In his statement Harwood described the lack of food, dysentery suffered by the prisoners, beatings inflicted by Muller, and other hardships. Muller was sentenced to six months' imprisonment.[20]

One of the POWs who received parcels from the depot was William Thomas Powell who was born in Birmingham in 1888 and lived in No. 68 Landsdowne Street. At the outbreak of war he was working as an artist in Saarbrucken where he was arrested on 5 August 1914. Powell was one of thousands of British civilians in Germany who were interned at Ruhleben camp, built on a disused racecourse outside Berlin, until the end of the war.[21] Whilst in the camp he painted a number of watercolours and drawings which he sent back to the depot in Birmingham. Some of these were displayed at an exhibition relating to Ruhleben camp held at Central Hall, Westminster in January and February 1919 to raise money for the Repatriated Prisoners Fund. The exhibition was visited by the king and queen and by the crown princess of Sweden who bought one of William Powell's works.[22]

After the Armistice the committee organised a series of entertainments in the Town Hall for all returning POWs. Here a meal was provided, various entertainers performed, and the lord and lady mayoress welcomed the men home.[23]

Endnotes

1 MS 466/1/1/15/3/11.
2 MS 466/1/1/15/3/11.
3 Report of Birmingham War Refugees Committee October 1915, Birmingham Institutions F/3.
4 MS 652/4.
5 MS 652/4; Report of Birmingham War Refugees Committee 1916, Birmingham Institutions F/3.
6 MS 652/6.
7 MS 466/1/1/15/3/13.
8 *The Southern Cross*, vol. 2 no. 13, MS 2046.
9 *The Southern Cross*, vol. 2 no. 16, MS 2046.
10 *The Southern Cross*, vol. 2 no. 17, MS 2046.
11 R0658-9 Mrs Naughton Dunn © Birmingham Museums Trust.
12 MS 946/11.
13 MS 466/1/1/15/3/46.

14 *Women Workers*, December 1914, pp. 83–4.

15 *Women Workers*, March 1915, pp. 100–1; June 1915, pp. 20–1.

16 *Women Workers*, June 1916, 16–17.

17 Branch Report, 1915, Birmingham Institutions A/6/529358.

18 All quotes from Scrapbook relating to Lady Mayoress' Depot, 1915-19, LF75.7/530991.

19 LF75.7/ 530991.

20 MS 1001/16-21.

21 http://ruhleben.tripod.com.

22 *The Times,* 30 January, 5 February, 11 February 1919.

23 *Women Workers*, December 1914, pp. 73–4.

3

A HIVE OF INDUSTRY

In March 1918, a group of national journalists visited Birmingham for a tour of the city's industrial contribution to the war effort. Although allowances have to be made for wartime propaganda, and their desire to keep up public spirits at a time when it was by no means clear that the outcome of the war would be successful, the journalists were obviously staggered by the scale of what they saw. As *The Times* reporter effusively put it:

> The tour has etched deeply on the minds of all who took part in it the picture of a city throbbing with energy directed to a single and unalterable purpose – the winning of the war … Birmingham and its environs form a vast mass of smithies and workshops, in which tens of thousands of men and women, boys and girls, are toiling night and day to manufacture military implements … We have been shown Tanks in course of construction – not one at a time, but by whole battalions … We have walked through miles of workshops and watched the manufacture of shells and fuses at all stages from the steel billet and rough brass forging to the finished and tested product. We have visited factories where rifles are made by the million and Lewis machine-guns by the thousand. We have inspected works which produce artillery limbers by hundreds. Monster aeroplanes have been built up under our eyes.

Aeroplane engines and big guns we have watched in the
making … What we have seen – and it is only a part of
the direct war work which is being carried out in this
area – has been a revelation. [1]

Despite the depression that initially struck local industry in the
first few weeks of the war, the recovery was rapid and by early
1915 Birmingham's huge industrial contribution to the war effort
was becoming a reality. Firms of various sizes were turned over to
government orders for the manufacture of munitions and other
war goods. Over the course of the conflict some 400 factories
and works across the city were involved in munitions, producing
a wide range of armaments including the Mills hand grenade,
which was invented in Birmingham and produced in hundreds
of thousands. Firms like Kynoch and Birmingham Small Arms
(BSA) extended their premises to cope with the demand and the

*Machine shop at
Kynoch Works.
(MS 1422/1)*

In 1914 BSA was producing 135 rifles and fifty Lewis guns a week. By the end of the war, weekly output was an average of 10,000 rifles and 2,000 Lewis guns. A total of 145,397 Lewis guns were produced during the course of the war.

number of people employed grew on an unprecedented scale. At BSA the workforce increased from 3,500 to 13,000. In 1914 the Austin Works in Longbridge employed 2,800 men, by 1918 it had a workforce of 20,000 and the size of the factory had grown immeasurably.

The war brought new initiatives as well. The National Shell Factory at Washwood Heath was established by the newly formed Local Munition Committee, which included the major manufacturers of munitions and labour representatives. The municipal Gas Department's Industrial Laboratory introduced a number of inventions including the production of toluol for high explosives and chrome steel as

Men of the Birmingham Repertory Theatre making munitions at Birmingham Aluminium Works, 1915.
Back row: John Dunn-Yarker, Claude Davies (in uniform). Second row (left to right): secretary of the works,
John Drinkwater (seated), Barry Jackson, Ion Swinley, Noel Shammon, W. Ribton Haines, Bache Matthews,
a foreman, a visitor. Front row: Felix Aylmer, E. Stuart Vinden, Ivor Barnard, Joseph Dodd. (MS 978)

WOMEN OF BIRMINGHAM
M–NITIONS O–TP–T
NEEDS
U and U & U
APPLY TO ANY EMPLOYMENT EXCHANGE TODAY

Printed for the Ministry of Information by Avery & Morris Ltd.

Recruitment poster for munition workers, c. 1915. (MS 4383)

a substitute for tungsten. Even Cadbury turned its production towards the war effort and branched out, at the government's request, into new experimental areas such as the drying of fruit and vegetables with new factories erected for the purpose.[2]

Although some men were exempt from joining the armed forces so they could work in munitions, the demand for workers in the city far outstripped the available workforce. This led to the most unlikely people working in munitions, including members of the Birmingham Rep, the theatre company founded by Barry Jackson in 1913. Some of the Rep's actors and staff had enlisted at the beginning of the war, including Scott Sunderland who enlisted in the Royal Warwickshire Regiment. During 1915 the male company members who remained worked every Sunday at Birmingham Aluminium Casting Company making shell casings, including the poet and playwright John Drinkwater and Jackson himself. Workers also came from elsewhere – Belgian refugees worked in local munition factories, there were about 250 Chinese workers in Birmingham 'doing work for which Englishmen could not be obtained', and by January 1917 there were also about 100 Australian munition workers in the city.[3]

The largest available body of potential employees was working-class women. Women working in industry was not a new phenomenon in Birmingham, as large numbers of women had been employed in various local trades and industries for many years. Their numbers increased during the war, and the range of work available to them was broader. They were also better paid than in the past although they were never paid on equal terms with men. Around 15,000 women came to Birmingham from all over Britain to work in munitions, and the numbers involved caused a housing crisis. A sub-committee of the Young Women's Christian Association (YWCA), led by Elizabeth Cadbury, co-ordinated the establishment of a munition workers' hostel in St Mary's Vicarage on the corner of Whittall Street and St Mary's Row. It had rooms for thirty-five women and most stayed a night or two before finding more permanent lodgings. It opened on 1 January 1916 and ninety-one women passed through its doors within two weeks, including a group of seventy from Jersey.[4]

Although the press made much of the middle classes entering the factories – an article in the *Weekly Mercury* on 5 August 1916, for example, described 'the daughter of a well-known Midland mayor at work on the lathe' – the vast majority of munition workers were working class.[5] There was great concern about the morals and welfare of these women, many of whom were young, and this, together with their high wages, received a lot of attention in the press. A number of welfare initiatives were put in place, designed to provide services for the munition workers whilst also exercising surveillance and influence over their behaviour. At a meeting on 2 November 1916, the lord mayor, Neville Chamberlain, described Birmingham as a 'veritable hive of munition workers', with young women drawn from 'the domestic-servant and shop-assistant classes' and subjected to long hours, fatiguing work, crowded lodgings, and the 'nervous strain of it all'. He proposed a Civic Recreation League to 'see that they did not come to harm, and to provide them with some alternative to the streets, the cinema, or the public house'. The Civic Recreation League provided moral and healthy entertainment including sporting and educational activities in a range of centres across the city.[6]

The female munition worker is one of the iconic images associated with the war. In Birmingham, women at work on munitions was the most-photographed aspect of the home front. The Library of Birmingham's collections include dozens of photographs taken for propaganda and promotional purposes by firms such as Kynoch.

Munition workers making Mills bombs at Mills Munition Works. (MS 4616/8)

Wartime crèches for the children of married munition workers were established at Trinity Road, Handsworth, Coventry Road, Sparkhill and Washwood Heath Road, Saltley by June 1917. Supported financially by the Ministry of Munitions and the local Education Committee, these were in addition to the two existing crèches in the city.[7] Canteens were formed, supported by voluntary workers – 'Edgbaston ladies' supported a canteen at Elliott's Metal Works in Selly Oak, the Women's Voluntary Reserve supported the canteen at Birmingham Metal and Munitions Works, and the Birmingham Women's Suffrage Society supported the canteen at BSA.[8] An article 'How I Solved the Dinner Problem' by 'A Munition Worker' in March 1918 described the fare that was available at the canteen run by the YWCA in Corporation Street. The sample menu included pea soup at three pence, boiled cod and parsley sauce at eight and a half pence, a savoury pasty at four pence, portions of potatoes, cabbage and swedes all at two pence each and stewed rhubarb and apples at two pence per portion.[9]

Locally manufactured aircraft were tested at Castle Bromwich Aerodrome, which was also a flying school for training pilots and support crew. Arthur 'Bomber' Harris was stationed there for a time during the war. There were a number of casualties in flying accidents at the airfield who are buried locally.

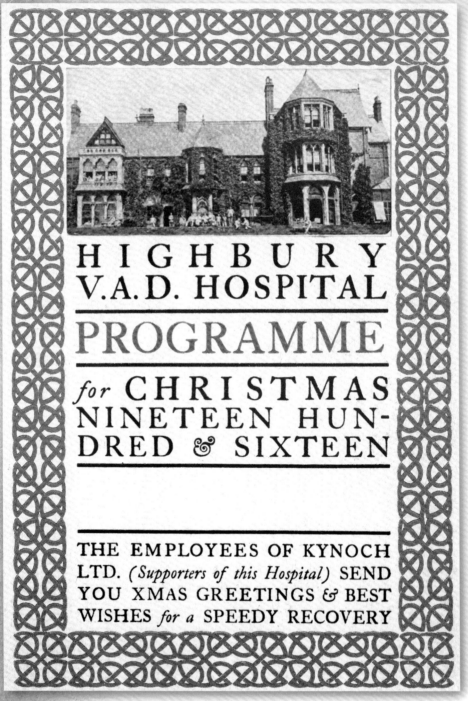

Programme for Christmas entertainment at Highbury Hospital, supported by the employees of Kynoch, 1916. (MS 4383)

Rest room at Mills Munition Works. (MS 4616/8)

BSA made much of the welfare programme that it put in place for its workforce. A small surgery had been established in 1913 for accidents and minor ailments and at the height of war production it received 400 visits from employees every day, with an average of five needing to be sent home or to hospital and six requiring a doctor. 'Lady Supervisors' were responsible for the health and welfare of the female workforce from 1916. From 1917 a scheme was introduced whereby every boy employed was examined by a doctor on entering the factory and his age, physical condition and level of education was recorded with recommendations for further training. There was a gymnasium with instructors for Swedish drills and gymnastics in the hope that 'the sound training and healthful habits now being inculcated will result in efficient workmen and useful citizens'. As many of the employees had to travel substantial distances to work, the new extension to the Small Heath Works built in 1914 included three canteens for men, women and 'staff', presumably office workers. The men's canteen sat 2,000, whilst the women's had seating for 750, and together they served 14,000 meals every twenty-four hours, including two meals during the night shift. A man could have 'a good helping of meat and two vegetables' for nine pence while 'girls' and boys were served a lesser portion of meat and vegetables for sixpence. Half a ton of potatoes was used daily and 250 gallons of tea were drunk every day.[10]

Whereas Kynoch and BSA operated at a vast scale, Edith Pittaway (later Warwood) recalled her work in a much smaller factory in an oral history interview with Birmingham Museum and Art Gallery staff in 1981. Edith was born in June 1892 at Minworth, the youngest of six children. After leaving school at 14 she became an apprentice dressmaker at Madame Howe's on the corner of Needless Alley and New Street. When her fiancé enlisted she left dressmaking to become a munitions worker at a small grenade-filling factory in Water Orton, where she worked from 1916 to 1918:

I thought I might just as well go and try and do something for the country and I went and of course they said that 'yes, you could start straight away', which I did. Now this factory was quite small and it was owned by a businessman by the name of Frederick Mountford and he had six or seven small sheds built, and it housed six to seven girls, no more than seven girls, each girl had to work in a little compartment by herself and these sheds, of course, were all wooden. We started work at this factory. We were working with TNT powder, a horrible yellow powder it was. First of all, I must tell you, we were provided with non-inflammable undercoat underneath, over which we wore a khaki overall and we also wore mob caps because we were warned that TNT powder would turn our skin yellow and we hadn't been working many days in the factory before we could see this yellow developing in hands and faces and it didn't distress us, really, we thought it would be something perhaps to be proud of and we went on working.

Edith was asked to take charge of a shed employing six or seven girls, and later transferred to more dangerous work involving detonators in a newly built part of the works which was referred to as the 'danger shed' or the 'rumbling shed'. A recollection of a visit by a Woolwich Arsenal inspector illustrates the dangerous nature of the work:

> Well, this girl, called herself an inspector, I suppose she was, she brought in a box of these tiny little detonators and she'd got to examine a percentage of these detonators. Of course I couldn't tell her what she was to do and she was examining these detonators. One day she saw one that looked as though it had a hair across it, just a fine hair. She tried blowing it, that didn't move it, she immediately took off her brooch and tried moving the hair and BANG! it exploded. It cut her finger down one side and of course that upset her very much.[11]

At the end of the war, like many munition girls, Edith lost her job and had to sign on the dole.

Munition workers at Water Orton, back row (left to right): Eva Mansell, Edith Pittaway (later Warwood), Marie Hunt, Mr Smith, Rosie Walker, Beatie Caldicott. Front row (left to right): Alice Picken, Edith Mansell, c. 1916. (MS 4116/8)

KYNOCH

Kynoch at Witton was extended in 1915 and spent over £2,000,000 on the plant during the war. An employment bureau was formed in 1915 to recruit the necessary additional workforce. It assessed the suitability of every woman and girl who applied, and found and inspected lodgings for them. 'Lady Superintendents' were introduced to supervise the women, the firm had its own ambulance, and rest and mess rooms were provided. By March 1918, Kynoch had 8,964 women in their employment, 1,298 of whom were described as undertaking work previously regarded as men's work. Of the 4,903 men still employed by the firm in 1918, over 900 had been medically discharged from the forces and 800 had been rejected for military service. At its height Kynoch in Birmingham employed 16,000, and had plants in Kynochtown, Essex, Arklow in Ireland and Umbogintwini in Natal, which employed 3,000, 2,390 and 2,320 respectively. In 1914, employees worked an average of seventy hours a week although this reduced to fifty-five by 1917 and 1918. The weekly wages bill increased from under £3,500 before the war to over £40,000 by March 1918. Annual sales figures before the war were about £1,500,000, compared to total sales of £55,063,370 for the four years ending in March 1918.

During the war Kynoch's contracted output every week was:

- 25,000,000 rifle cartridges
- 700,000 revolver cartridges
- 5,000,000 cartridge clips
- 110,000 18-pounder brass cases
- 300 tons of cordite

Output peaked in 1918 when 29,750,000 cartridges per week were produced as part of a special effort to meet the demands of the German offensive.

The workforce paid a weekly subscription from their wages to equip and maintain hospitals for wounded soldiers at Highbury and at Moor Green House. Over the course of the war the Kynoch workforce subscribed £40,000 towards the cost of the hospitals.

Munition worker at Kynoch Works. (MS 1422/4)

During the war, Wolseley Motors in Adderley Park, a subsidiary of Vickers, produced over 4,000 military vehicles, 4,500 aero engines, and 700 completed aeroplanes, as well as firing gear and gun-sights for 300 warships.

As well as their expanded role in industry, the war saw the employment of Birmingham women in a number of other jobs that were previously closed to them. In transport, women replaced men as conductors and cleaners on the trams from July 1915, and although they were not allowed to drive, the jobs were very popular as they were paid the same as men – a highly unusual situation. In August 1915 the local press deemed the 'Lady Tram Conductors' to be a 'huge success'.[12] They also worked as ticket collectors and cleaners on the railways from Spring 1915. There was a large increase in women performing clerical work particularly for the city council, which saw 7,000 of its male employees enlist, and in the postal service. Women also worked in street cleaning, tarring road surfaces, in manual work at the Gas Works, and as gardeners at Cannon Hill Park.[13] Although Birmingham was an urban area, there were a few local women who joined the Women's Land Army to work in agriculture, co-ordinated from 1916 by the Birmingham War Agricultural Committee. Women also often had to keep a husband or son's business going whilst he was away, and in Handsworth Mrs Matthews of No. 3 Queen's Head Road kept her husband's chimney-sweeping business afloat during his absence.[14]

Men were also replaced by young boys who had yet to reach military age. The Birmingham Scouts were very active during the war: about 450 scouts worked as bellboys on trams in their spare time, built huts for soldiers, worked for the Public Works Committee whitening kerbs and lamp posts in parks, helped with air-raid precautions, and over 300 of them served at coast-guard stations on the East and South coasts. In October 1916, Birmingham Fire Brigade had two young firemen, W.J. Jones aged 16 and A.R. Tozer, the son of Birmingham's chief fire officer, aged 17.[15]

Children participated in the war effort in large numbers and many of their activities were co-ordinated by their schools. Schools became sites in which children were trained in civic and national duties as citizens in time of war. The school logbook

Mrs Owen, a postal worker during the war. (MS 4616/4)

can be a rich source demonstrating how the conflict influenced the school's culture and the children's day-to-day experience of education. The school curriculum could become a site for expressing patriotic feelings. Throughout the war, Mr Tipper at Dartmouth Street Boys Department delivered a regular programme of lectures beginning in November 1914. Topics covered included 'Patriotism (Empire)', 'The Landing of the Indian Troops', 'Colonial Gifts to the Motherland', 'Compulsory Service (Derby Scheme)', 'The Waste of War (Young Lives)' and 'The Future (Social Problems & War)'.[16]

Children also took an active part in fundraising for a number of causes. In City Road School they raised funds for the Prince of Wales' Fund, for Belgian refugees, Serbia, the YMCA Hut Fund, wounded soldiers and sailors, and regularly sent gifts of eggs, fruit, chocolates and walking sticks to the 1st Southern General Hospital. They also gave concerts to entertain the wounded at Dudley Road Hospital.[17] Between August 1914 and June 1919, the children of Dartmouth Street collected over £50 for various war charities, a significant amount of fundraising which must have represented a considerable drain on most families' budgets.[18]

The teaching staff in local schools was severely disrupted as male teachers left for the front, often to be replaced by female teachers, and the school day had to be reorganised to deal with staff shortages. Considerable attention was focused on former teachers and pupils who were at the front. In November 1916, the boys of Bristol Street Council School sent Christmas parcels to two former teachers, Mr Hopkins and Mr Smith, who were in France.[19] On 7 December 1916, the logbook of Clifton Road Boys School records 'Great enthusiasm among present pupils & teachers' on dispatching twenty-two more parcels containing scarves, cigarettes, socks and mittens to soldiers and sailors who were old boys.[20] Girls were engaged in sewing and knitting comforts for the front, and the girls of Oakley Road School knitted socks for soldiers during their playtime.[21]

November 1915 saw great excitement at Dartmouth Street School when the press announced that former pupil Arthur Vickers had been awarded the Victoria Cross. The head teacher

A First World War knitting party. (LF75.7/530991)

addressed the school, 'cheers were given; and the medal saluted as the boys passed out'. On 3 December 1915, the school held a 'V.C. Day' when a half-day holiday was given in honour of Vickers who visited the school. The head wrote 'The V.C. was given a most enthusiastic reception by the boys and staff (2 p.m.). The Head Teacher congratulated him on the distinction he had won and assured him of the intense pride which the School felt in him.' Vickers addressed the boys and thanked everyone for the 'hearty reception'. In June 1919, Vickers again visited the school when the boys and staff presented him with a 'handsome Smoking Cabinet as a permanent token of their pride in and admiration for his gallant deeds during the Great War'.[22]

Many of the pupils had fathers and brothers at the front, and visits by former pupils enabled the boys to learn more about what they might be going through. On 25 August, City Road

School Boys Department was visited by Lieutenant Hague of the Royal Engineers who had been badly wounded in the lower jaw and left shoulder; whilst on 30 September, Corporal Harold Whitehouse of the Royal Warwickshire Regiment – wounded in the Dardanelles – addressed the senior boys and girls, and returned to the school the following day for the whole of the afternoon to continue his talks to the pupils. In November 1917, Private Arthur Smith, a teacher at the school, visited during his first absence from the front for eighteen months and 'had some interesting talks with the Children on "Life at the Front"'. Smith returned to the school's staff after a period as a prisoner of war in March 1919. [23]

The school could also become a focus for collective mourning, and expressing grief and loss. In September 1917, Harry George Tipper, head teacher of Dartmouth Street

The youngest investor in Birmingham Tank Bank Week 31 December 1917– 5 January 1918. (LF 75.7/531718)

School Boys Department, recorded that 'it has been my painful duty to announce to the school the death in action of a number of old scholars: where possible recent letters have been read, and photographs of the school's dead heroes have been placed in the corridor'.[24] From October 1914, the head teacher of City Road School, John Adams, used his school logbook as a way of acknowledging former pupils who receive distinctions, and memorialising those who were killed in action. He had a very personal interest in the war as his only son was serving at the front. On 12 March 1915, the children and staff had 'wished goodbye and Godspeed to 2nd Lieut. Ralph Adams' of the 1/8 Battalion Royal Warwickshire Regiment who returned to visit the children on 26 October whilst home on leave 'after 8 months in the Trenches'. Ralph was educated at King Edward's High School and the University of Birmingham before going to work for the brewers Mitchells and Butlers. On 14 January 1916, John Adams proudly recorded that Ralph had been awarded the Military Cross. On 20 September 1916, Ralph was awarded a bar to his Military Cross for 'conspicuous gallantry during a raid on the enemy's trenches' but was reported wounded and missing since 1 July when he was last seen leading his men into an enemy trench. It was not until 9 February 1917 that John Adams received official notice from the War Office confirming that Ralph had been killed on, or soon after, 1 July 1916. In July 1917 a framed photograph of Ralph was hung in the school hall.[25]

However detailed the school logbooks, they are, of course, written by the adult teacher and don't therefore represent the children's own voices. Some schools had magazines that were written and edited by the children, and where they survive they provide an insight into the opinions and thoughts of children and young people at the time. *The Cradle* was written by the boys of Allcock Street Council School. Two 13 year olds, Kenneth Sutherland and Harry Phipps, edited the issue for October 1914, illustrating how they had fully absorbed patriotic messages about duty and responsibility. Copies of the magazine were sent to former pupils who were serving in the trenches:

We are afraid our readers hardly realise what serious times we are living in. The greatest War in History is being fought closer to us than a good many imagine. Really the scene of battle is only a few hours distant. What, perhaps, brings the War closer to us than anything else is the fact that 266 of our boys have relatives fighting for us. Some, alas! have lost their fathers or brothers and quite a number have some one wounded. To them all we extend our deepest and heart-felt sympathy. The question arises, 'What can we do to help?' We cannot fight but we can do what is asked of us cheerfully and lighten the care cast on our mothers' shoulders. When we think of the fathers, brothers &c. lying in the trenches we are sure no Allcock St boy would disgrace himself by giving trouble at home. Now and always, the watchword must by 'Duty'.

On 13 November 1915, the *Birmingham Weekly Mercury* ran a children's competition on the theme 'What can the Little Ones do in War Time?' and half a crown was offered for the best letter. First prize was awarded to Irene Harrison (age 13) from No. 145 Ladypool Road, Sparkbrook, one of six children of a widowed mother. Her winning entry was published on 20 November:

Denial is a great sacrifice, and it would bring a smile to many a soldier's face if he had a cigarette that was bought with our pennies that were saved each week instead of being squandered at the sweet shops. 'Tommy' would treasure a scarf, a pair of gloves, knitted pair of socks or a helmet; he would think more of them if bought and knitted with our small hands, for every soldier has not a sweetheart, wife, or mother; lots of them, given the title of 'The Lonely Soldier,' never receive parcels from relations like their chums do when away from their home; the simple reason is because they have no friends or relations. Would not it be nice to feel that we have got a friend who is a big red-faced soldier?[26]

A further selection of letters was published on 27 November, and like Irene, the authors advocated duty and sacrifice. Stanley Eld, the 13-year-old son of a commercial traveller in jewellery, living at No. 69 Somerset Road, considered it to be 'absolutely necessary that we should be well equipped to take the fallen's places either in business, professional, or commercial careers … by just studying hard and keeping fit I am convinced we shall be doing our bit'.[27] Mary Nicholls, age 10, of No. 147 Vicarage Road, Aston, advocated buying British goods and knitting for soldiers, 'One of the first things I think little children should do is to make up their minds that they will not purchase anything made by Germans or Austrians, for by doing so they are helping the enemy. At the Vicarage-road School girls like myself are taking home wool to knit socks to send to our soldiers.' Several focused on Belgian refugees, Leslie A. Harris, age 12, of No. 141 Ladypool Road, Sparkbrook, argued that 'Most boys and girls could afford a halfpenny or a penny every week to help this excellent cause … When one thinks about it one realises that the Belgians deserve it, because if it had not been for their bravery and courage the Germans may have been pillaging England the same as they did in Belgium.'

Harold Collins, the 13-year-old son of a builder from No. 48 Newport Road, Balsall Heath suggested that 'Some boys interested in wood-work could make picture frames and brackets which they could sell and give the proceeds to war funds', whilst Albert J. Harris, of No. 31 Eton Road, Sparkbrook, thought girls had a particular role, presumably influenced by some of the recruiting posters which appeared at the time; he thought that girls should 'help the recruiting sergeants by trying to persuade the "slackers" to enlist voluntarily while they have the chance'.

The war had a profound impact on family life as sons, brothers, husbands and fathers were absent from home for long periods of time and many did not return. The impact on families where the father was a single parent could be severe, particularly after conscription was introduced in 1916. The Citizens' Committee took responsibility for the care of soldiers' children who were temporarily or permanently without a mother and therefore had no parent at home when the father enlisted. During 1916 it undertook the care of 270 children, of whom 266 were the children of soldiers.[28] The records of Middlemore Emigration Homes include cases where the committee called on Middlemore to house the children. On 17 January 1916, for example, they visited a sister and brother aged 12 and 9 years old respectively, who were both described as 'exceedingly small for age, and poorly clad'. Their mother had died and their father was now serving as a private in the Kings Royal Rifles. Before leaving England he had handed over the care of the children to the Citizens' Committee until he returned. They were accepted into the homes temporarily as 'Not for emigration'. The girl was released into the care of a local woman by the committee on 28 June 1917, whilst the boy was reclaimed by his father after he was demobilised on 26 April 1919.[29]

Endnotes

1   'War Activities of the Midlands (I)', *The Times*, 25 March 1918, p. 5.
2   *Bournville Works Magazine*, 1917, pp. 203–5.
3   *Birmingham Post*, 6 August 1917, p. 4; 29 January 1917, p. 3.
4   *Women Workers*, March 1916, pp. 112–14; MS 466/1/1/15/3/13.
5   *Birmingham Weekly Mercury*, 5 August 1916, p. 3.
6   *Women Workers*, December 1916, pp. 83–6.
7   *Women Workers*, June 1917, pp. 9–11.
8   *Edgbastonia*, August 1915, p. 527.
9   *Women Workers*, March 1918, 104–6.
10 George Frost, *Munitions of War: A record of the work of the B.S.A. and Daimler Companies during the World War 1914–1918* (Birmingham and Coventry: The B.S.A. Co. Ltd and Daimler Co. Ltd, 1919).
11 R0087 Edith Warwood © Birmingham Museums Trust.
12 *Birmingham Weekly Mercury*, 28 August 1915, p. 1.
13 *Birmingham Weekly Mercury*, 18 March 1916, p. 1.
14 *Birmingham Weekly Mercury*, 18 March 1916, p. 1.
15 *Birmingham Weekly Mercury*, 7 October 1916, p. 1.
16 S56/2/2.
17 S48/1/1.
18 S56/2/2.
19 S36/1/1.
20 S50/2/1.
21 *Birmingham Weekly Mercury*, 19 June 1915, p. 6.
22 S56/2/2.

23 S48/1/1.
24 S56/2/2.
25 S48/1/1.
26 *Birmingham Weekly Mercury*, 20 November 1915, p. 6.
27 *Birmingham Weekly Mercury*, 27 November 1915, p. 7.
28 E.M.R. Shakespear, 'Birmingham Citizens' Committee',
    Women Workers, March 1917, pp. 97–105.
29 MS 517/A/8/1/4; MS 517/A/8/2/2.

4

WRITING HOME

It was not only children who were affected by wartime separation; married life was also disrupted by long absences. Like other family ties, relationships were sustained by writing letters. Alice May Tottman married Howard Harrison in 1915 and after their marriage they lived in No. 23 Botteville Road, Acocks Green. Howard served as a private in the Machine Gun Corps. He wrote very affectionate letters to Alice, conveying how much he missed her and how he longed to come home. On 5 June 1918 he wrote:

> I hope Dearie you did not mind me asking you to leave the platform before my train went out. It wouldn't have been much good if youed [*sic*] have stayed as I was in the corridor. Then again these partings do not help to cheer our lives. I felt as though Id not left you & somehow couldnt believe I was travelling away from you. I do hope this horrid business will not last long its too much for us both.[1]

Similarly, on 2 August 1918 he wrote, 'I've been thinking quite a lot of you today Dearie but as usual it makes me long to be with you. We must carry on Old Girl & make the best of things. Like you I hope the business will soon finish.'[2] Less than a month later, on 2 September, Howard Harrison was killed in action in France age 31. After his death Alice left Birmingham and moved to Wales.

Wedding of Howard Harrison and Alice May Tottman, 1915. (MS 2682/4/6)

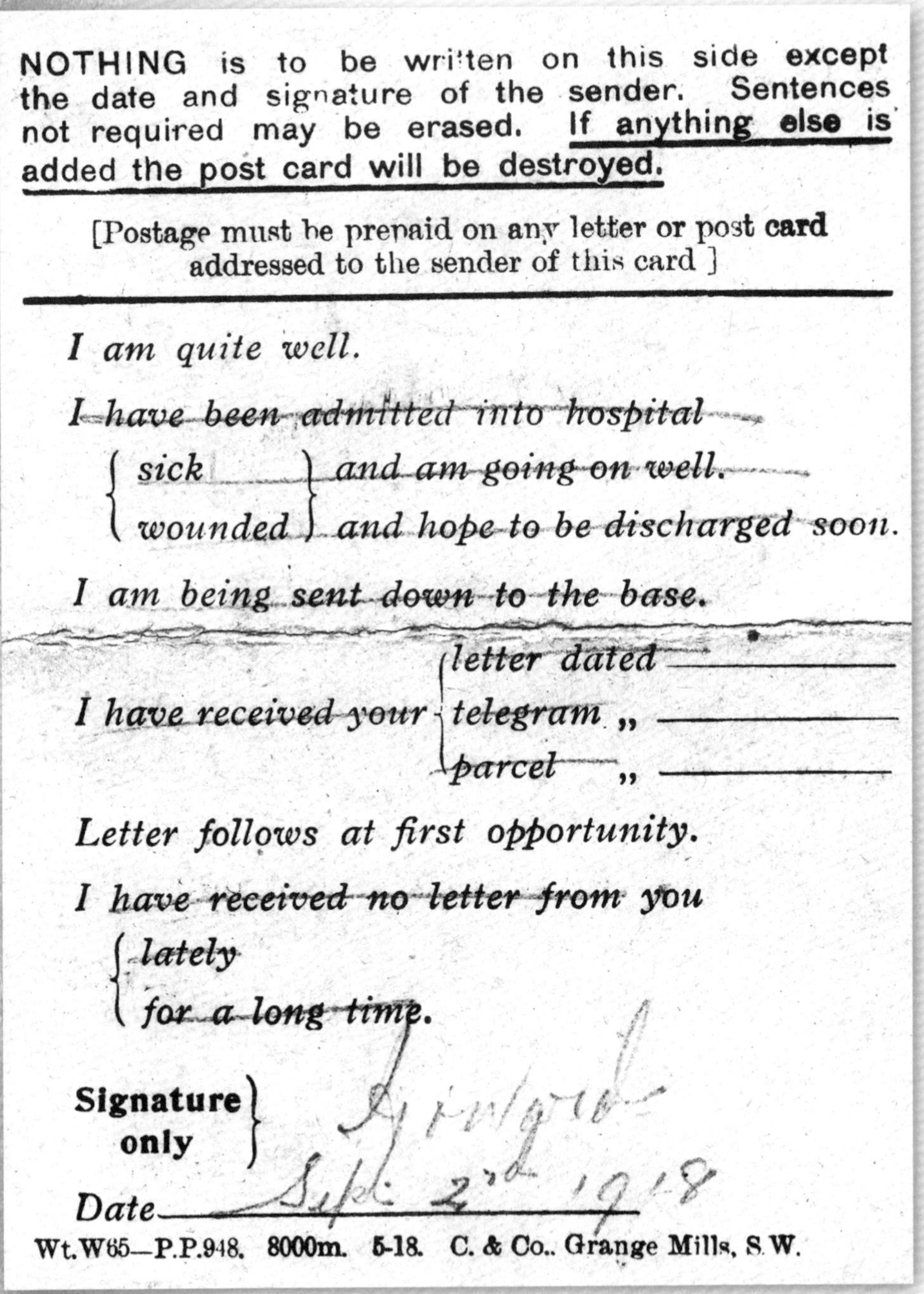

NOTHING is to be written on this side **except** the date and signature of the sender. **Sentences** not required may be erased. **If anything else is** added the post card will be destroyed.

[Postage must be prepaid on any letter or post **card** addressed to the sender of this card]

I am quite well.

I have been admitted into hospital

{ sick } and am going on well.
(wounded) and hope to be discharged soon.

I am being sent down to the base.

I have received your { letter dated ———
telegram „ ———
parcel „ ———

Letter follows at first opportunity.

I have received no letter from you

{ lately
(for a long time.

Signature } *Howard*
only }

Date *Sept 2nd 1918*

Wt.W65—P.P.948. 8000m. 5-18. C. & Co.. Grange Mills, S.W.

Field postcard from Howard Harrison to Alice, 2 September 1918. (MS 2682/1/15)

Men also wrote to parents, and to their brothers and sisters. Joe Irwin, a private in the machine-gun section of the 1/6th South Staffordshire Regiment, wrote regularly to his sisters Olive, who lived at No. 20 Evelyn Road, Sparkhill, and Gert who lived in Wolverhampton. The letters describe his life in the trenches and Olive regularly sent paper to Joe with her parcels of food so that he could write home. Joe was at pains to reassure his sisters that he was well and was always glad to receive letters and parcels from home, particularly food and cigarettes, explaining on 11 April 1915, 'I am always glad when I get a parcel from home as I get things that I cant get out here', before assuring everyone that he was 'going on alright' but they had seven men killed during a spell in the trenches and about a dozen wounded.[3]

Joe Irwin, c. 1914.
(MS 4669)

Joe employs inventive ways to communicate his location without offending the censor; in one letter, for example, he tells them that he was in 'a place where a lot of fighting has been done we were in the same trenches as those that played the Germans at football on Christmas day'. On 13 May 1915, he sends Olive 'a little forget me not from out of the firing line they grew in a garden of a farm right by the trenches we are in'. The pressed flowers survive with the letter, as does the pansy he sent Gert in a letter on 26 March. Joe survived the war despite being wounded in June 1916.

Christian Creswell Carver was born in 1897, the son of a prosperous brewer living in Harborne. He served in the Royal Field Artillery and was a prolific writer of regular letters to his parents and his younger brothers. At 10.30 p.m. on 10 May 1917, he wrote to his brother Humphrey, or 'Hump' as he called him, from 'A nasty dug-out' in which he complained of being 'bored to extinction'. He went on to describe the former German dugout from which he was writing, beginning on a light note before turning to reflect on how he felt the war had changed him:

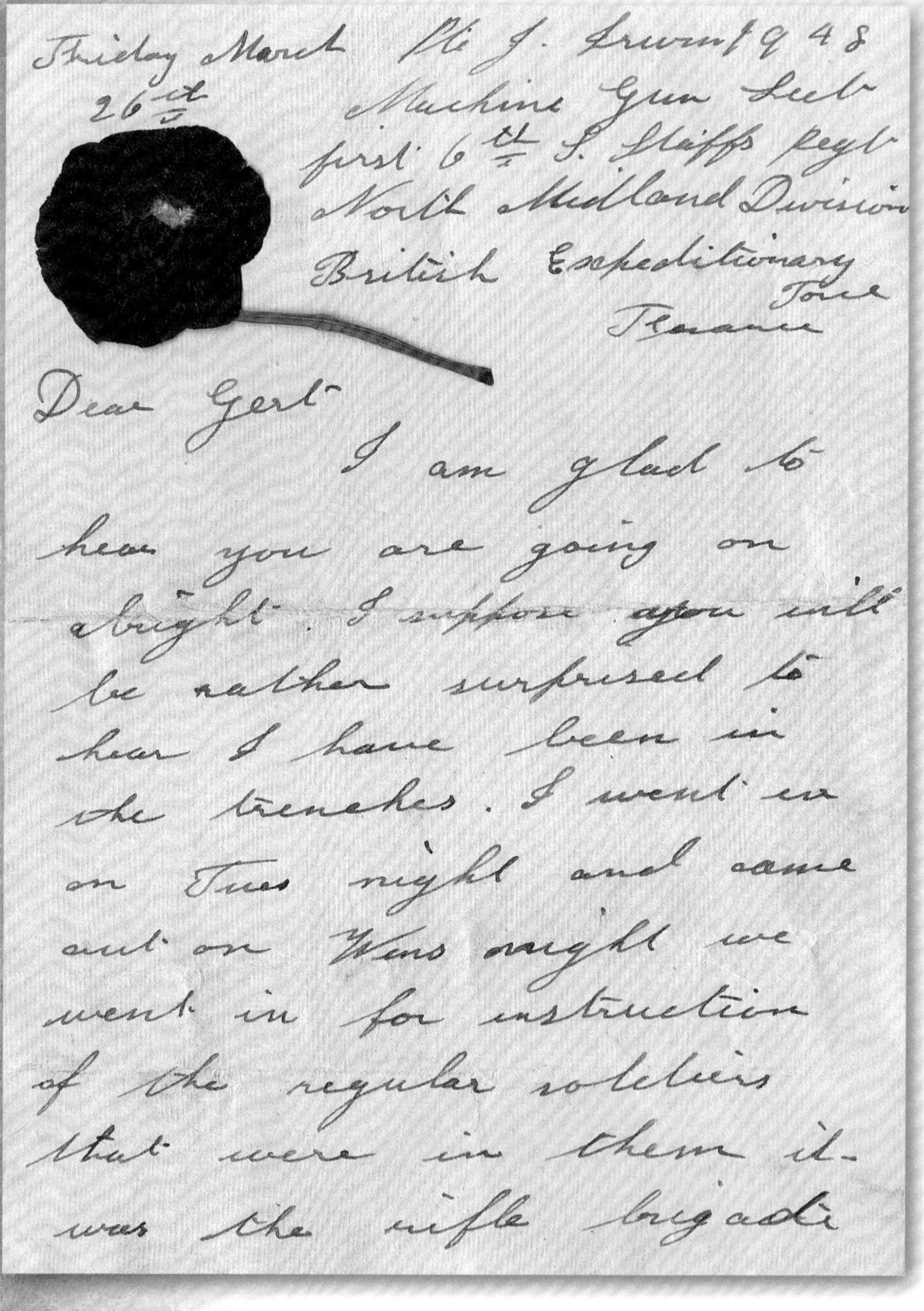

Friday March Pte J. Brown 9 4 8
26th   Machine Gun Sect
first 6th S. Staffs Regt
North Midland Division
British Expeditionary
                        Force
                    France

Dear Gert

        I am glad to
hear you are going on
abright. I suppose you will
be rather surprised to
hear I have been in
the trenches. I went in
on Tues night and came
out on Wens naight we
went in for instruction
of the regular soldiers
that were in them it
was the rifle brigade

Letter from Joe to Gert with the dried pansy that he sent from France, 1915. (MS 4669)

Christian Creswell Carver on his BSA motorbike whilst on leave, January 1916. (L78.1)

This particular burrow is inhabited by a cat, left behind by the boche when he departed in haste. It has recently become the proud mother of a considerable family, who are the subject of some controversy. What nationality are they? They were born of a German mother, on French soil, and in an English colonel's tin hat. Upstairs a number of booms, crashes and shakes indicate the Ger. idea of fun. He gets a lot of that sort of fun, though. What a crooked, topsy-turvy time. Now I was made to be a thinker rather than a doer, a dreamer, an idealist say, not a man of action. Everything went as per schedule till I was 18, and since then I have tasted danger and adventure, and much as I dislike it sometimes, yet life without it would seem hopelessly dull. In fact after the war, I feel certain that I could not enjoy a peace existence without occasional little wars, expeditions up the Amazon and to the North Pole and so forth. I only hope they will be forthcoming. A melting pot in very truth. We men are hurled into the cauldron of war and emerge as something different. Restless, fierce, with the lust of adventure, a perpetual unrest in our blood. I can feel that I have been through the moulding process. For a long time I merely disliked war, the ugliness, the dirt, the blood, and I was horribly frightened of shells. Now I don't particularly mind shells, and I enjoy the work and the danger and all this great game of chance and skill.[4]

Christian was killed in action in July 1917 and was buried in Lijssenthoek Military Cemetery in Belgium.

About 150,000 Birmingham men and women served in the forces during the war, a figure that for men represented some 54 per cent of the military-age adult male population of the city. Some 35,000 men came back disabled and over 13,000 never returned.

Victoria Cross

The Victoria Cross is the ultimate recognition for bravery on the field of battle. Thirteen men who were either born in Birmingham, or who had close connections to the city and spent considerable parts of their lives here, were awarded the Victoria Cross during the war. Their place of birth was Birmingham unless stated otherwise.

- Second Lieutenant Herbert James, 4th Battalion Worcestershire Regiment, at Gallipoli on 28 June 1915.
- Private Arthur Vickers, 2nd Battalion Royal Warwickshire Regiment, during an attack at Hulluch on 25 September 1915.
- Private Thomas George Turrall, 10th Battalion Worcestershire Regiment, at La Boiselle on 3 July 1916.
- Sergeant Alfred Joseph Knight, 2/8th Battalion London Regiment, at Alberta Section, Ypres, on 20 September 1917.
- Flight Lieutenant Alan Jerrard, No. 66 Squadron Royal Flying Corps, near Mansuè, Italy, on 30 March 1918. Born in London but moved to Sutton Coldfield as a child.
- Sergeant Norman Augustus Finch, Royal Marine Artillery, HMS *Vindictive*, at Zeebrugge on 22–23 April 1918.
- Sergeant Albert Gill, King's Royal Rifle Corps, at Delville Wood on 27 July 1916. Killed in action, 27 July.
- Lance-Corporal George Onions, 1st Battalion, Devonshire Regiment, at Achiet-le-Petit on 22 August 1918. Born in Bilston.

- Acting Sergeant Harold John Colley, M.M., 10th Battalion Lancashire Fusiliers, during a counter-attack at Martinpuich on 25 August 1918. Killed in action, 25 August. Born in Smethwick.

- Lance-Corporal Alfred Wilcox, 2/4th Battalion, Oxford and Buckinghamshire Light Infantry, near Laventie on 12 September 1918.

- Lance-Corporal William Amey, 1/8th Battalion Royal Warwickshire Regiment, during the attack on Landrecies on 4 November 1918.

- Acting Lieutenant Colonel James Neville Marshall, Irish Guards attached to 16th Battalion Lancashire Fusiliers, during the attack on Sambre-Oise Canal near Catillon, 4 November 1918. Killed in action, 4 November. Born in Manchester.

- Acting Major Arnold Horace Santo Waters, 218th Field Company Royal Engineers, while bridging the Sambre-Oise Canal on 4 November 1918. Born in Plymouth.

Men did not just write to their families, they also wrote to employers and former colleagues. Several employees of W. Canning & Co. Ltd enlisted early in the war and the firm's archive includes a remarkable series of letters from almost thirty of them in which they give a detailed picture of their lives during the long periods spent in reserve and the shorter spells in the trenches. They touch on several themes which are common to many of them, including boredom, discomfort and danger, and seem particularly keen for their readers to understand their experiences. The importance of a connection to home, to their workplace and workmates, and to Birmingham comes through particularly clearly. Bill Veisey, unlike many of the Canning men, wasn't in the Royal Warwickshire Regiment but served in the North Staffordshire Regiment. On 17 April 1915, however, he wrote of how he'd been looking out for the Warwicks and had finally caught a glimpse of them:

> The Warwicks are pretty smart – well of course, they come from the right place, its funny how proud you get of your native town – when you are out of it. But I get too thirsty when I begin to write about Brum … You must understand that the water is undrinkable until it is boiled or filtered in the water cart with a few tons of chloride-of-lime (ugh) so fellows are compelled to drink beer instead when they can get it, which aint very often, with about as much effect. No it certainly isn't up to M & B's standard.[5]

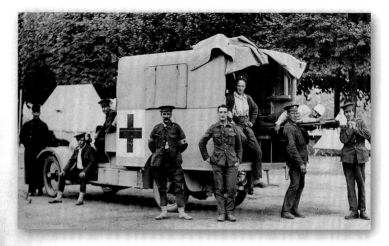

A British ambulance made by Wolseley at Angers, 1914. (MS 1676/17)

Like the other men, he didn't spare those at home from the consequences of war and some of the sights that he saw. On 2 May 1915 he described the wounded:

> The fighting has been very severe this last week and several thousands of wounded have passed our place in motor ambulances. We arnt [*sic*] far from the line & it's a sight to see the cars loaded up with poor fellows all covered with blood. They seem to get hit mostly on the head or legs, its most peculiar. The Indian troops nearly always get wounded in the hands, as they have got a habit of catching of the enemy's bayonets when they make a charge … Thank you very much for your very kind offer to send me something by post, Its really very good of you, sir & I should be very pleased to accept anything.[6]

Several of the men describe the physical discomfort and provide vivid accounts of the weather and the conditions in which they lived and served. Private J. Sturch, 1/5 Royal Warwickshire Regiment wrote on 19 August 1915:

> Just a line to let you know I am going on alright & am in the best of health. We have just come out of the trenches for eight days rest, we have had it a bit rough this time, we have been up to our waist in water, the trenches are in a terrible state, on Sunday night August 8th it thundered & lightend & rained for hours & we had to be in it all the time, because at times like that the germans [*sic*] are liable to attack us the lightening was flashing on our bayonets it's a wonder there was not any struck by it & all the time I have been in, I have had to go about the trenches without any trousers on or socks, & we could not get a shave or a wash till we came out, eight days without a wash or a shave, I did feel in a state, we even had to make tea with rain water, what we had drained into a sapp, the smell of the trenches are awful,

there are dead bodies everywhere, even buried in the parapet were [sic] we fire from, & the rain has washed the soil off them & we have had to bury them at the back of the trench.[7]

The importance of food and receiving regular parcels from home to keep up morale is another constant theme. Lance Corporal Percy R. Postlethwaite, who served in the 9th Battalion, Kings Royal Rifles, wrote on 26 August 1915: 'Thanks ever so much for the ripping box of Tuck which I have just received.

Turner and 'A little comic business with a periscope (Life Guard One!), J2 Arras', March 1916, photographed by J.A. Wall. (MS 4616/3)

'Toilet! Company Head Quarters K1 Arras', June 1916, photographed by J.A. Wall. (MS 4616/3)

Charles A. Bill and Turner, Front Line J1 Arras, March 1916, photographed by J.A. Wall. (MS 4616/3)

Really the cake & sardines are absolutely topping and a darn good bit better than bully beef & biscuits.'[8] A few days later, on 30 August, he wrote again and after explaining how 'letters from home are so welcomed out here', went on to describe a new chemical weapon which the Germans had developed which he thought would be of interest to his former colleagues whose work at Canning also involved chemicals:

Soldier wearing gas mask. Image taken from the papers of Lance-Corporal James Henry Allcock, King's Royal Rifle Corps. (MS 1816/2)

By the way it may be interesting to know that the Germans have still another chemical invention which they have tried to use on us. It is in the form of a shell fired by their ordinary artillery and when exploding pours large clouds of dust on you. This dust is similar in many respects to Red Ochre with a result of burns should any rain or spots of water get to it. Ha! Ha! Judging from the time we have been out here we seem to have fared pretty well for German inventions don't we? A few of things we have undergone are asphyxiating gases (including gas shells which injure your eyes), shells which explode several times, boiling tar, liquid fire, aerial torpedoes, and the above mentioned shell, which throws out a burning powder. By jove don't I wish I could use some of W.C. & Co's chemicals on them.[9]

However, the men were not in the trenches all the time and spent considerable periods in the reserve lines where they experienced the lighter side of life. As at home, football was a popular pastime and, on 29 April 1916, Corporal Harold Rose of the Army Ordnance Corps described a recent game:

> I have managed to get an evening & an afternoon off for football this week & as the weather is very warm indeed at present football is a bit out of season. We had a 10 mile journey for a match on Thursday last & although we lost, we had a good tea so that more than balanced matters. Our fellows had played this team before & on the quiet I think it was on the strength of getting a good tea, that we played them again.[10]

In Chapter 1, we encountered Harold W. Perry of the 1st City Battalion. Writing on 22 December 1915 from France, he conveyed his initial shock on the conditions of their 'trench "Baptism"':

> The first night we were there was a bit of a shock to us as we were in a firing trench standing in liquid mud nearly up to our waists with German shells and 'Whizz-bangs' flying over our heads. The impression I got was that I was watching a firework display under extremely uncomfort-able conditions. Certainly some of the 'Fireworks' came a little too close to be pleasant … Well, cheer ho! every-body, we are proud to be doing our 'bit' and are looking forward to the time when we shall make our triumphant return to Brum.[11]

Harold went on to distinguish himself and wrote on 8 June 1916, describing the action in which the 2nd City Battalion had been involved:

> The 2nd battalion were the worst sufferers again during a very heavy bombardment of our trenches a week ago. Trenches & dug-outs were blown in & a number of men

View of no-man's-land taken from a listening post, Maricourt, January 1916, photographed by J.A. Wall who also noted 'white in distance is Bosche line'. (MS 4616/3)

buried alive. We were in the support line at the time & were rushed up with picks & shovels to dig them out. The fire was so intense however that we were unable to get to work & were ordered to return. We lost a few men coming back but we brought them down the trench. I had a very narrow escape & experienced a queer feeling when a whizz-bang shell dropped into the trench 2 yards in front of me & failed to explode. 'For this relief much thanks' I said to myself as I started off again.[12]

In early September 1916 he was wounded in the shoulder but by 17 September he was back at the front and described an attack on Falfemont Farm when his company captured forty prisoners and some machine guns:

In this attack we had to charge a distance of 250 yards over ground torn by shells and swept by machine gun bullets, but our boys never wavered and when our objective was reached, went for them with a yell. The only prisoners we took were those who took refuge in dug-outs and these men did not need telling twice when we shouted to them to come

Captain J.A. Wall of the 3rd City Battalion recorded his war photographically. He was a former pupil at King Edward's School, Birmingham and was wounded on the Somme in September 1916. The photographs on pages 24, 88, 89, 90 and 93 are from two albums he compiled.

out of it. I went to one dug-out with the captain's revolver in one hand and a bomb in the other, and when I had fired a couple of shots down, a voice shouted up 'Mercy, English'. Knowing their treacherous nature I was doubtful whether to take them prisoner or finish the lot of them off, but noticing a few of them were wounded I took the risk and called down 'Allemands vorwaerts'. Up they came, seventeen altogether, looked very scared and sorry for themselves, and after I had collected their wrist watches, rings and helmets for distribution amongst the boys I sent them off with an escort. Of course we did not come through this little lot without losses and after the fighting was over I found myself in charge of the Company.[13]

He went on to report that his captain had recommended him for a VC for putting a machine gun out of action. He did not receive the VC but was awarded the Distinguished Conduct Medal with which he confessed himself 'naturally somewhat disappointed'.[14]

Private Reginald Smith of the Royal Warwickshire Regiment writes particularly colourful accounts of his experiences in France. Reg was a clerk at Canning and the son of Mrs Rosena Smith of No. 25 Varna Road, Edgbaston. He is one of several men who refer to the justness and importance of the cause for which they are fighting, reinforcing to himself and others why he enlisted, however uncomfortable and dangerous the experience might be. On 20 May 1915, he took issue with some of the reporting of the conflict in the press:

I saw in the papers that we have a picnic out here – it is no picnic – its just grim work that has to be done & we are all determined to do our duty to the end. It is quite a popular falacy [sic] at home that the Germans are bad shots. I shouldn't care to show my head above the parapet for a few minutes & their trenches are two to three hundred yards off ours … Still we don't mind doing these things because we know they've got to be done & it is for the best cause in the world.[15]

X mas Greetings
7th Division
1917
Ypres
Neuve Chapelle
Festubert
Givenchy
Loos
The Somme · The Ancre
Écoust-Croissilles
Bullecourt
Passchendaele Ridge

Christmas card from the papers of T.R. Sutherland, 1917. (MS 771/5)

By 3 November 1915 the weather was having a detrimental effect on the trenches, which he described as 'in several places knee deep in mud and water'. The local wildlife also left quite a bit to be desired, although it did provide some rather ghoulish entertainment: 'The rats here have a most annoying way of crawling over you whilst you are lying down – asleep or not – they are about as big as kittens, but we derive great amusement and sport through them, by trying to bayonet them. When you become an expert one can get quite a decent bag.'[16]

On 12 November 1915, Reg wrote a particularly vivid account of his exploits from near the village of Fonque-Villiers, some 12.5 miles south of Arras, after explaining that he was giving the letter to a 'fellow on leave to post … so that the censor wont be able to use his pencil on it'. He described the ruined village, only 800 yards from the German first-line trenches. Reg had a narrow escape when his clothing was damaged by a German bullet, but took great delight in getting his own back:

I have nearly met with disaster myself here – in fact they did go as far as ruining a pair of my trousers, by, putting a bullet hole through 'em – whilst I was in 'em too – and the annoying part about it was that I hadn't another pair – consequently I noticed the slightest draught all day. Vowing vengance [*sic*] I marched up to the firing line – the casualty to my trousers occurred in the village – and taking a nice position between two sandbags – waited for the first head to appear over the parapet. In about 10 minutes a fellow in the near of their lines stepped out of a trench to hang up a shirt he'd been washing so I let drive at once – I missed him but he turned and ran for cover quite smartly – leaving his shirt on the line. I peppered that shirt for a good half hour and one or two more of our fellows did the same. I'll bet it's more draughty than my trousers if he's wearing it now.

Like the others he regularly tried to convey his experiences to those at home – of how loud the ongoing noise of the artillery was, and how he felt when under fire from some of the weapons used by the enemy:

However they have got opposite us, a most annoying imple-ment which they use for throwing Aerial Torpedoes – now the name doesn't convey much to you but I can assure you the sound of one bursting conveys quite a lot. Its really disturbing to have one burst within 30 or 40 yds of you. The only thing in the way of sound that I have to equal 'em was the mine they exploded in front of our trenches at Ploegstraat. You can imagine perhaps what they are like when I tell you that they make a hole 6 yds deep – put a couple horses & carts in the hole comfortably. They caught a working party of the 7th Batt one night and dropped one on them – 3 or 4 fellows couldn't be found at all and the remainder (there were about 12) they put in sandbags – of course they were blown almost to bits – they went to lay the remains of one poor devil out and found out that they'd put two hands too many in his sandbag. Yes I must really own to a decided antipathy towards 'aerial torpedoes'.[17]

On 4 May 1916, Reg's brother wrote to inform the firm that he had been wounded by a shell in the arms, leg and abdomen on the previous Saturday night, and although he was taken to hospital he died of his wounds at 12.30 p.m. on Sunday – his twenty-fifth birthday.

In addition to writing letters home some men, particularly officers, recorded their experiences in detailed diaries. Captain Arthur Impey related his wartime activities in a diary covering the period between August and November 1918 when he was involved in the British advance from Albert to Maubeuge. Impey came from a well-known Quaker family in Northfield and served in the 79th Brigade, Royal Field Artillery. In his diary, Impey described the actions in which he was involved, his colleagues and friends, and wrote lyrically about the countryside in which he found himself. On 3 September he described an encounter with the enemy, an example of a small act of humanity between men of different armies:

> Men served in the front-line trenches for an average of seven days. After that they would be relieved and transferred to reserve trenches where they might still be called upon to reinforce the front line if necessary. When at rest they would be billeted away from the front line.

Whilst we were eating, the servants came in & said they had found a wounded hun, so I went to have a look at him, & found him about a hundred yards away, lying by a quite fresh shell hole with a badly broken leg, a bullet through the knee. He was a fine looking fellow, an NCO, with red beard, & speaking a little french told me he was a maching [*sic*] gunner, & had been hit the day before by a stray bullet, about 5.0pm & had lain there ever since … He was a good fellow, hadn't lost his nerve, and was most dignified, neither cringing nor arrogant. I went back and told the others, and was more than a little tickled to see I [his colleague], whom I had so often heard swear, in awful terms that no death was bad enough for Hun machine gunners, to whom no quarter should ever be given – take him with his own hands a cup of tea & Bully beef & bread & butter, our lunch in fact, which the poor devil wolfed without a word, & the last we saw of him was being carried off by some of our stretcher bearers who turned up, the very picture of the vanquished, but by no means dishonoured enemy.

In the decades after 1918 some men published autobiographical accounts of their war service. Charles A. Bill, seen here (on the left), published *The 15th Battalion Royal Warwickshire Regiment (2nd Birmingham Battalion) in the Great War* in 1932. It describes the battalion's military action in battle and daily life in the trenches.

Captain Impey's diary ends with the declaration of peace. He spent 10 November 1918 wondering what was going on, 'No news, and no Orders, No one knows where the Huns are … No Whisky left – played bridge till bed time.' On the 11th he was still waiting for news:

No news first thing so after Breakfast I wandered into the Village, and met some of our 17 Div Infantry marching back. I asked them where they were going to, and someone said 'Home' they looked rather happy, and I wondered if it could be true. Then an extraordinarily rubicund and happy looking Brigadier trotted along. I asked him if it meant Peace, he said 'Yes, I've just been talking to the Corps, its official' so I went back to the battery, and told the Sergeant Major to fall the men in, in the Orchard. They all seemed to know what it was, and fell in in a hollow square, grinning & expectant. Just as I was going to tell them, an orderly appeared with a message, which said 'Hostilities will cease at 11.00 Hours' so I read that. Nothing much happened, they cheered, not wildly, we all felt it to be so very unreal and in a short time they were back at work, cleaning Harness and Guns and grooming the Horses. After lunch I rode over to call on Mac. who was in a comfortable Estaminet, a mile the other side of the Village, a cheery crowd there, Straafer, Torrence and Ore and we played bridge. A quiet evening and early to bed.[18]

Endnotes

1 MS 2682/1/8.
2 MS 2682/1/12.
3 MS 4669.
4 *Christian Creswell Carver* (Birmingham: Privately Published, 1920), pp. 306–7, L78.1, also available online at http://ww1centenary.oucs.ox.ac.uk/bookmark/ christian-creswell-carver-university-of-oxford/
5 MS 2326/1/26/1.
6 MS 2326/1/26/2.
7 MS 2326/1/23/2.
8 MS 2326/1/12/2.
9 MS 2326/1/12/3.
10 MS 2326/1/18/8.
11 MS 2326/1/9/5.
12 MS 2326/1/9/6.
13 MS 2326/1/9/12.
14 MS 2326/1/9/13.
15 MS 2326/1/19/4.
16 MS 2326/1/19/6.
17 MS 2326/1/19/7.
18 MS 3498.

5

Determination and Dissent

By 1917 life on the home front was getting harder. The long lists of casualties and worrying news compounded the weariness that people felt after two and a half long years of war. There was still a demand for news from the battlefront and local venues such as the Gaiety, the Grand and the Hippodrome made use of the relatively new technology of film to satisfy the demand. In December 1916 the Grand Theatre showed *With The Empire's Fighters*, a film by Hilton DeWitt Girdwood, which featured battlefield scenes and charges by the Gurkhas. Girdwood was

Indian soldiers in front of a transport wagon made by Wolseley in France, 1915. (MS 1676/17)

attached to the Indian Government and the local press reported that he had therefore 'naturally given the native troops from India a prominent position, and quaint and picturesque scenes from the daily life of our Indian regiments are shown'.[1] Birmingham saw itself as a leading city of the Empire and there was widespread local interest in 'Indian troops' with numerous articles and photographs in the local press from 1914 onwards. The *Birmingham Post* reported a visit to the city by a party of Indian officers on 22 January 1917, when they were received by the lord mayor in the Council House and then toured various munitions factories.[2]

> Over 1.3 million men served in the Indian Army, a tenth of the British Army. Many were Muslims and Sikhs from the Punjab. Indian troops arrived on the Western Front in September 1914. Among the battles in which they fought were Ypres, Neuve Chapelle, the Somme and Passchendaele.

Local theatres and music halls kept up a steady stream of performances throughout the war and were popular with the home-front population and with servicemen on leave. The Rep Theatre continued to produce plays throughout the war and the company also performed for the wounded. In October 1915 the theatre hosted a concert of Indian plays and music to raise money for wounded Indian troops, and in June 1916, the Rep gave an open-air performance of *Twelfth Night* for the patients of the Southern General Hospital.[3] In 1917 the Rep courted controversy when it staged John Drinkwater's play *X=O: A Night of the Trojan War*. Although set in the Trojan War, it featured four soldiers discussing the folly of war. Despite considering it 'the best play Mr Drinkwater has given us yet' the *Birmingham Mail* deplored its production and went on to comment that 'Mr. Drinkwater has plainly been deeply stirred by the war; but out of all the glories and horrors, of the last two-and-a-half years the one impression made upon his mind is that war means that young poets, artists, dreamers, heroes of both sides shall mutually exterminate one another in a conflict in which they have no real interest over a paltry quarrel long since lost sight of. He is apparently oblivious of all that England went to war for … Therefore we think he was very ill-advised to put it forward at present.'[4] Later the same year Drinkwater left for France to entertain the troops with Lena Ashwell's Concert Party.

MUSIC DURING THE WAR YEARS

Popular music associated with war took many forms and fulfilled several purposes including:

- National anthems and songs of Britain and her allies
- Songs in support of those allies
- Songs in support of the armed forces
- Songs the troops sang
- Instrumental medleys of these songs
- Patriotic marches and other descriptive piano pieces

Music served to increase patriotic fervour, reflect recruitment drives, improve morale at home and abroad, and to connect people with the armed forces. Song sheets were produced with vivid covers: stirring, evocative, dramatic as required. In some cases music was used to raise money for the war effort (at both a local and national level) and this is reflected in the Library of Birminham's collections. For example, W.A. Brookes of No. 44 Oxford Road, Acocks Green wrote and published 'Britannia's Glorious Flag' with music by his son Edward. Dedicated to 'the officers and men of the Royal Warwickshire Regiment', every copy sold benefitted war funds including The Belgian National Relief Fund, the Indian Soldiers' Fund, and the *Weekly Dispatch* Tobacco Fund.

Classical composers contributed to the war effort in varying ways. Elgar wrote several pieces in support of Belgium at the beginning of the war. In October 1917 the first complete performance of *The Spirit of England* was given in Birmingham: this 'war requiem' (which included three of Laurence Binyon's poems) was dedicated by Elgar to 'the memory of our Glorious Men'. Vaughan Williams spent much of the war as a stretcher-bearer (despite being overage). Arthur Bliss, E.J. Moeran, Ivor Guerney, George Butterworth, and Ernest Farrar all served in the armed forces, and Butterworth and Farrar were killed in action. Those who survived were often profoundly affected by the war and used music to give voice to their feelings in the following years.

Cover of the song sheet for 'Britannia's Glorious Flag'.
(Music Songsheets Reference Collection)

One of the issues that caused disaffection was the shortage of food. Securing an adequate supply was a problem throughout the war but from 1917 it became a serious issue. Queues outside food shops became a regular sight, and the Schools' Medical Officer complained that children were being kept off school to wait in food queues. The Citizens' Committee organised lectures on war economy and food, and in February 1917, it opened a War Economy Centre in the Windsor Arcade where cookery demonstrations were held. The situation became so grave that the lord mayor, David Brooks, established a Food Committee in March 1917.

Thrift became a way of life and 'Economy in Waste' leaflets were distributed through schools and other organisations. Old tin cans were collected and recycled, householders were asked to gather waste paper, and even offal from slaughterhouses was repurposed as food for pigs and poultry or as fertiliser. There was an increased emphasis on growing more food, particularly as 1917 saw a serious shortage of potatoes. The city's Parks Department made more allotment plots available and supplied seeds at reduced prices. By the end of the war, about 1,800 acres of land in the city was covered by allotments.

In August 1917 the Government Food Controller requested that all local authorities appoint food control committees, and the lord mayor's local committee was put on a statuary footing. The committee introduced a registration scheme for all outlets selling sugar and ration cards for sugar were introduced in September 1917. Butter, margarine, tea and bacon were also in short supply. A general rationing scheme was tried in Birmingham as an experiment and from 12 December every house in the city received a ration card for tea, sugar, butter and margarine. A similar card was introduced to ration meat, with an extra portion allowed for men who were engaged in heavy manual work. The Birmingham trial later became the basis for the rationing scheme that was introduced nationwide in July 1918.

Fuel had been in short supply since 1916 when the then lord mayor, Neville Chamberlain, established a Coal Purchase

Food queues, 1917.
(MS 4616/1)

Committee to address the shortage of coal. The cold winter
of 1917 made the situation worse and a system for coal
rationing was introduced in 1918, which again involved the
registering of all suppliers and consumers. These problems
did not disappear with peace. Food shortages and high prices
continued, the Birmingham Food Control Committee was not
disbanded until June 1920 and the coal shortages continued
well into 1920.

Although the city appeared to be a hotbed of pro-war enthusiasm, it had also been home to a lively pacifist opposition to
the war from the very beginning. Birmingham had a small but
highly influential Quaker community which included families
such as Cadbury, Lloyd, Sturge, Southall and Albright, whose
members were prominent among the civic and business leaders
of the city. Quakers had a long-standing commitment to peace
and during the war many risked unpopularity, public censure,

City of Birmingham Refuse Disposal Department

ECONOMY IN WASTE.

WHAT THE CORPORATION ARE DOING.

BY-PRODUCTS produced from house refuse reduce the City expenditure.

TIN CANS, etc., are stripped of their coating of tin, then pressed into billets to be melted and used again.
The tin also recovered is very valuable.

WASTE PAPER is sorted, bundled, and sent to paper makers to be re-made into clean new paper, saving hundreds of tons of paper to the country in a year.

MANURE for your gardens is made from the refuse of the meat and fish markets.

GREASE from waste meat is used for candle making, also for lubricating purposes.

PIG FOOD & POULTRY FOOD are made from waste meat and butchers' refuse.

The foregoing items are of National Importance at this time of crisis.

CLINKER, i.e., the remains of the refuse after cremation in the Destructors, is used for making roads, garden paths, concrete, mortar, sewage filter beds, etc.

CONCRETE PAVING FLAGS are also made from clinker.

WHAT THE PUBLIC CAN DO.

REDUCE the quantity of refuse to be removed by not putting the following into the dust bin :—

GARDEN REFUSE.—Bury it in your garden, or better still burn it; the ashes are a valuable manure. In either case your garden will benefit.

GRASS CUT FROM GARDEN LAWNS. Arrangements should be made with the nearest Horse or Cattle owner for a twice-weekly collection of grass cuttings from lawns.

POTATO AND FRUIT PARINGS, AND OTHER VEGETABLE WASTE, if clean can be used for soups.
Are also valuable food for Pigs and Poultry, either your own, or your neighbours'.
If not used thus, should be burnt on the Kitchen fire.

RAGS.—Woollen and Cotton Waste should be put on one side for the Lady Mayoress' Scheme in aid of the Red Cross and other War Funds.
If voluntary workers do not call, a postcard to the undersigned will ensure collection.

WASTE PAPER should be tied with string and placed on the top of the dust bin, or
If you have a large quantity, a post card will bring a bag to your house and ensure collection.
May also be taken to our Depots (for prices see handbills).

CINDERS should be riddled from ashes and used again on the fire.—There is a shortage of Coal.

SLOPS, LIQUID REFUSE, AND TEA LEAVES MUST NEVER be put in the dust bin.

HOUSEWIVES!

Here is a unique opportunity to help yourselves, your City, and your Country, by observing the above Rules.

THESE FIGURES WILL SURPRISE YOU:

The Domestic Refuse collected in the City of Birmingham exceeds **700 tons per day,** or **200,000 tons per year.**

If **EVERY HOUSEHOLD** reduced the refuse thrown into their dust bin by 1 lb. per day (only 7 lbs. per week), the reduction throughout the City would exceed ... ... **30,000 tons per year.**

This would make possible a saving of over ... ... **£13,000 per year.**

The Council House, Eden Place, Birmingham.
May, 1917.

S.D. 28900.

JAS. JACKSON, Superintendent.

Handbill advising on recycling and war economy, May 1917. (MS 4383)

and imprisonment for their beliefs. The British Committee of The Hague Congress included a handful of Quaker women from Birmingham – Geraldine Southall Cadbury, Maria Catharine Albright, the American-born co-warden of Woodbrooke Mary Braithwaite, and her sister-in-law Ethel C. Wilson also of Woodbrooke. Geraldine, her daughter Dorothy, Catharine Albright, Mrs Harrison Barrow and Florence Barrow all wanted to attend The Hague Congress but, like almost all the British women, they were refused permission to travel.[5]

A number of peace meetings were held in the city throughout the war. On Christmas Eve 1916, a peace meeting was held in the Bull Ring when a procession of women walked from a prayer meeting in the Priory Rooms to be addressed by Miss Haly. A similar meeting was held on New Year's Eve. On 29 July 1917, Margaret Haly also organised a peace meeting on behalf of the Women's International League and the Fellowship of Reconciliation; the meeting was held in the Bull Ring as part of the national Women's Peace Crusade. The local press reported that a crowd of about 300 assembled in Old Square and marched to the Bull Ring. Haly, who was referred to as 'a well-known local suffragette', presided and the principal speaker was Helen Crawford of Glasgow.[6]

Not all Quakers were anti-war, and there was a tension between those who believed this war to be justified, or at least the lesser of two evils, and those who took an absolutist pacifist stand. A third of young Quaker men of military age enlisted and served in the armed forces during the war, and members of prominent local Quaker families such as the Cadburys, Lloyds, and Impeys, took very different attitudes to the conflict. Egbert Cadbury, or Bertie as he was known, was the youngest son of George and Elizabeth Cadbury and a student at Cambridge in 1914. He joined the navy and served on the HMS *Zarefah* and later HMS *Sagitta* before transferring to the Royal Naval Air Service. Despite this he was welcomed

The war divided women's suffrage campaigners. Mrs Pankhurst (Women's Social and Political Union) and Mrs Fawcett (National Union of Women's Suffrage Societies) supported the war. A pacifist group split from the NUWSS and helped organise the controversial Women's Peace Congress at The Hague, 28 April–1 May 1915.

Postcard relating to the potato shortage, 1917. (MS 4067)

at his local Quaker meeting when home on leave, and his mother Elizabeth wrote in her journal on 5 October 1914 that 'Bertie was surrounded at Meeting by all the members congratulating him and talking to him; it was quite difficult to get away'.[7] After training at Hendon he was stationed at Great Yarmouth and flew his first mission against German Zeppelins on 9 August 1915. He wrote lively letters home describing life at the station and the very long hours. On 19 September 1915, he described what happened during a 'Zepp. scare':

On about five successive nights now, just as we were sitting down to dinner, a Zepp would be reported approaching the coast somewhere in our beat. Result – a general panic. All the pilots jump into cars and dash down to the sheds, closely followed by all the mechanics in lorries. As our way is right along the front, several cars and two 4 ton lorries loaded with men hurtling down to the Air Station frighten the whole of Yarmouth. On arriving down there our machines are put on the Denes and engines tested – perhaps some unlucky fellow is sent up to do a patrol, the night being as black as pitch. Then starts the most nerve-racking process I know. We all sit round the fire in the Officers quarters down there like so many doomed men. Suddenly with a nerve-shattering roar the telephone rings and an Officer is wanted imme-diately on the 'phone. Someone dashes to it the rest sitting round in a deathly silence trying to read the message by the look on the said officer's face. Then a tremendous sigh of relief when his face lights up and he announces that the Zepp. is travelling North, East, South, or West, anywhere but towards us. Or the other thing – sickening roar of engines, everyone getting hopelessly rattled and up go the machines, racing backward and forward along the coast, searching the sky or the depths beneath them for any signs of enemy activity.[8]

On 28 November 1916, Bertie came to prominence nationally in a widely reported exploit in which he shot down a Zeppelin and received the Distinguished Service Cross. In August 1918, and now a captain in the RAF which had been formed in the April of that year, he was awarded the Distinguished Flying Cross for bringing down what was reputedly the last Zeppelin to attack Britain.

Bertie's elder brother Laurence took a different course as one of the founders of the Friends Ambulance Unit (FAU) in August 1914, an alternative form of service for Quaker men of military age who did not want to join the army. The FAU could be a dangerous alternative – another Birmingham Quaker, Colin Priestman, died on 8 August 1918 whilst collecting the wounded at the front. Laurence served in France and was awarded Officer of the Order of the British Empire, and received the Croix de Guerre from the French Government. Despite their different paths the brothers remained close, as their letters to each other preserved in the Cadbury Research Library demonstrate. In fact, Bertie became disillusioned, particularly after one of his best friends was killed in an air accident, and railed in his letters against stay at home decision makers, whilst Laurence agonised over whether to join the army.[9]

Egbert (Bertie) Cadbury in his aeroplane. (Bournville Works Magazine, November 1915)

Satirical cover for a FAU smoking concert programme, Dunkirk, August 1915 (MS 4039)

It was a different story in the Lloyd family where, as Judy Lloyd demonstrates in her detailed study, the dilemmas faced by young Quaker men prompted a family crisis.[10] Gertrude and John Henry Lloyd were devout Quakers and had four sons – Alan, Eric, Gerald and Ronald. The family occupied a prominent place in Birmingham's civic life; John Henry was a well-known businessman running the family firm Stewarts and Lloyds, and a city alderman who had served as lord mayor in 1901. Their second son Alan Scrivener Lloyd enlisted almost immediately and was given a commission as Temporary Second Lieutenant in the 78th Brigade, Royal Field Artillery. He married Dorothy Hewitson on 1 September 1914 and, after eight months' training, left for France. Alan was driven by patriotism and a desire to prove himself, he also wished to distance himself from his family's Quaker religion and pacifism, and quarrelled with his parents over his decision to enlist. Alan was killed on 4 August 1916 at Ypres when his son David

Ronald Lloyd in his FAU uniform, December 1914. (MS 4039)

was 10 months old. A letter in the family papers from his fellow officer, R. Julian Yeatman, described how they were mending a telephone wire when they were hit by a shell. Yeatman went on to describe 'the gallant disregard of the most obvious danger by your son on this and all other occasions of this kind … a gallantry that amounted almost to recklessness'. Alan was posthumously awarded the Military Cross.

In the interim Ronald and Eric had both joined the FAU. After training at Jordans in Buckinghamshire, Ronald left for Dunkirk on 30 October 1914 as part of the first FAU party to leave England to render first aid to the sick and wounded under the banner of the Red Cross. His brother Eric followed on 23 December. A hospital was established in the Villa St Pierre at Malo les Bains, Dunkirk, and the ambulance work at the front developed rapidly. Ronald increasingly felt guilty that he was not 'doing his bit', a feeling which strengthened after Alan's death. On 1 December 1916, his mother wrote to him after he had confided some of his reservations to his parents; his brother Eric had already left the FAU and joined the navy:

Page from an autograph album belonging to Anna Goulding, May 1917, reflecting the social pressure to enlist. (MS 1465/13)

We have just received your letter of Nov 24 & it makes my heart sink & ache. Oh my darling am I to lose you too … I can see you want dangerous work but oh my Ron can't you find any without joining the Army & going into the Artillery? I must not urge you against your conscience but oh my son do pray over this very very carefully, and please do nothing hastily …

Ron continued to struggle with his conscience. Finally he wrote home on 22 August 1917 saying, 'I think I ought to join. My reasons are the same as before, only stronger. I feel I've no right to continue this ambulance work and that I'm not doing my proper share.'[11] Ronald left the FAU on 20 December 1917 and enlisted with the Royal Field Artillery. The war ended before he got to fight and he returned to his parents' home in Birmingham. Gerald, the eldest brother, remained a pacifist throughout the war and undertook alternative service with the YMCA looking after their huts for soldiers. Family anecdotes related that he was presented with white feathers in the street. Eric, Ronald and Gerald survived the war and remained Quakers throughout their lives.

Although men had been under serious social pressure to enlist from the beginning of the war, the introduction of conscription in 1916 brought matters to a head. In fact, despite the initial enlistment fervour in Birmingham and the formation of the City Battalions, recruitment was spasmodic in the first few months of 1915. Lord Mayor Bowater led a special recruitment appeal in May which saw a short-term rise in numbers to about 600 volunteers a week, but which again dropped off by the autumn. A national register was compiled in August and September, which indicated that there were a large number of single men of military age who had not enlisted voluntarily. From November 1915 the 'Derby Scheme', named after Lord Derby the director of recruiting, required men aged between 18 and 41 to 'attest' or pledge that they were willing to be called up to serve. Single men were to be called up before married men. By the end of November, 3,000 men a week were enlisting in the city and Birmingham fulfilled its target of 30,000 by the end of 1915. Still more men were needed, however, and conscription was finally introduced in early 1916.

Local men who did not enlist due to age or working in a protected occupation could join the Home Defence Corps of volunteers, who would undertake duties such as guarding munition factories and in the case of an enemy invasion would

5th Battalion Warwickshire Volunteer Regiment, 'B' Company

Officer Commanding, CAPTAIN C. S. YATES.

Headquarters, 558 Coventry Road, (entrance Charles Road).

INVASION OF ENGLAND

FIELD-MARSHAL LORD FRENCH and other high Military Authorities have recently declared that

There is a great possibility of an attempted Invasion of England,

and therefore they have urged upon **EVERY MAN the duty of preparing himself** for such an emergency.

It is better to be
PREPARED and not Wanted !
than to be
WANTED and Not Prepared.

Come and join the SMALL HEATH COMPANY,

Any Evening from 8 p.m. to 9-30 p.m., at the above address.

M. Dighton, Smallheath Printing Works.

have formed the last line of defence. The Small Heath Home Defence Corps, later known as B Company 5th Battalion of the Royal Warwickshire Volunteer Regiment, included a member of Birmingham's small black population who is shown in photographs of the corps in 1917 and 1919. His name was Frederick Johnson although we know little more than that about him.

Like elsewhere a local tribunal was established in Birmingham in January 1916 under the terms of the Military Service Act which lasted until July 1919. It dealt with 90,721 cases, of which 34,760 went to the army and 7,749 received exemption certificates, only nine of which were absolute, the others being temporary or conditional exemptions. By March 1916 conscientious objectors

Small Heath Home defence Corps, c. 1917. (Birmingham Scrapbook, vol. 10)

who refused both military service and alternative service were being arrested and court-martialled, and several Birmingham conscientious objectors were subsequently imprisoned. Men who refused to be conscripted were subjected to criticism and huge social pressure. The *Birmingham Weekly Mercury* of 15 April 1916 included a photograph of two small boys who had turned up at the Curzon Hall to enlist. One of the boys was given a pair of goggles to wear and the paper reported that although he 'was proud … their desire was for khaki suits'.[12] While this illustrates the influence that being surrounded by information about the war effort and recruitment propaganda could have on children, it also served as a dig at those men who were opposed to being conscripted.

A number of leading local Quakers were conscientious objectors and they worked closely with other anti-conscription organisations such as the No Conscription Fellowship. Wilfred Littleboy, a Birmingham chartered accountant and assistant clerk of Warwickshire North Monthly Meeting, was imprisoned in 1917. He was taken first to the guardroom at Budbrooke Barracks in January 1917 and later to Wormwood Scrubs. In all he was imprisoned for twenty-eight months and not released until 1919. The Quakers' pacifist stance resulted in many coming under suspicion. On 6 November 1916, the police visited the homes of four local Quaker magistrates – William A. Albright, Harrison Barrow, Joseph Sturge and George Cadbury – and presented them with a list of ten questions designed to test their loyalty. They also requested to inspect their chequebooks to see whether they had donated money to anti-conscription organisations.[13]

Not all conscientious objectors were motivated by religion. Oliver William Benwell was a schoolteacher at Stirchley. On 6 June 1916, he had to report to the military authorities and was subsequently imprisoned. He was brought before a tribunal at Wormwood Scrubs Prison and in the statement he presented to the tribunal he explained his reasoning:

Small boys attempting to enlist at Birmingham recruitment office. (Birmingham Weekly Mercury, 15 April 1916)

I have a moral (though not religious) objection to taking combatant service. I have not the decided opinion that it is morally wrong to take human life under all circumstances. There may be occasions when such action would be justifiable … It does not follow, however, that it is my moral duty to go and kill my fellow men because I am commanded to do so by those in authority over me. I have the moral right to decide whether I shall fight or not, and no man has the moral right to compel me to kill if I feel that I am not justified in doing so.[14]

From November 1916 he performed alternative service with the 4th Southern Company of the Non-Combatant Corps (NCC) at Chiseldon Camp, Wiltshire. The NCC, referred to in the press as the 'No-Courage Corps', was established in March 1916 as part of the Army Reserve; its members were uniformed privates who did not carry weapons or fight but undertook physical labour in support of the military. Conscientious objectors assigned to the NCC as alternative service were often treated harshly by the officers. In May 1918, Oliver was sentenced to two years' hard labour for disobeying an order when he refused to maintain a rifle range. He was imprisoned in Winchester where he remained until June 1919. After the war Oliver was lucky in that he had a sympathetic head teacher and he returned to teaching at Stirchley School on 1 September 1919.[15]

The Military Service Act became law in January 1916 and introduced conscription in Britain. It allowed exemption on grounds of religious or moral objection to fighting, and tribunals were established to deliver judgement on exemptions. Nationally there were 16,500 conscientious objectors. Most undertook alternative service: 985 refused and were imprisoned.

Many on the political left also opposed the war, and were particularly opposed to conscription, which they perceived as contrary to fundamental British civil liberties. Things were far from simple, however, and the local labour movement was divided over their attitudes to the conflict. The Birmingham Trades Council voted to oppose the introduction of conscription and this resulted in a split between the anti-war faction and a 'patriotic Labour' group, which included well-known and

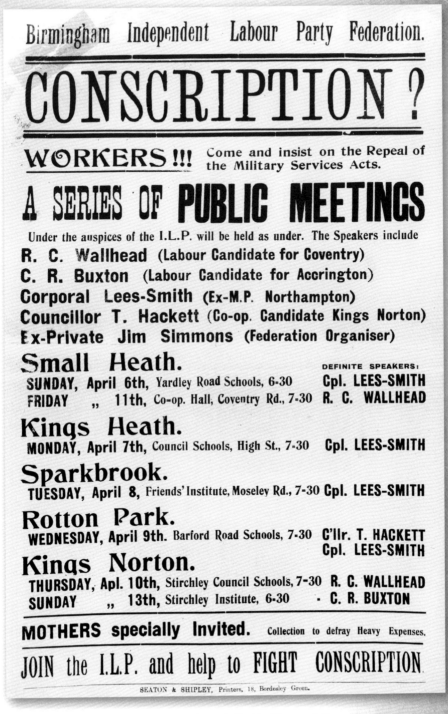

Birmingham Independent Labour Party Federation.

CONSCRIPTION?

WORKERS!!! Come and insist on the Repeal of the Military Services Acts.

A SERIES OF PUBLIC MEETINGS

Under the auspices of the I.L.P. will be held as under. The Speakers include

R. C. Wallhead (Labour Candidate for Coventry)
C. R. Buxton (Labour Candidate for Accrington)
Corporal Lees-Smith (Ex-M.P. Northampton)
Councillor T. Hackett (Co-op. Candidate Kings Norton)
Ex-Private Jim Simmons (Federation Organiser)

Small Heath.

DEFINITE SPEAKERS:

SUNDAY, April 6th, Yardley Road Schools, 6-30   **Cpl. LEES-SMITH**
FRIDAY ,, 11th, Co-op. Hall, Coventry Rd., 7-30 **R. C. WALLHEAD**

Kings Heath.

MONDAY, April 7th, Council Schools, High St., 7-30 **Cpl. LEES-SMITH**

Sparkbrook.

TUESDAY, April 8, Friends' Institute, Moseley Rd., 7-30 **Cpl. LEES-SMITH**

Rotton Park.

WEDNESDAY, April 9th. Barford Road Schools, 7-30 **C'llr. T. HACKETT**
 Cpl. LEES-SMITH

Kings Norton.

THURSDAY, Apl. 10th, Stirchley Council Schools, 7-30 **R. C. WALLHEAD**
SUNDAY ,, 13th, Stirchley Institute, 6-30 - **C. R. BUXTON**

MOTHERS specially Invited. Collection to defray Heavy Expenses.

JOIN the I.L.P. and help to FIGHT CONSCRIPTION.

SEATON & SHIPLEY, Printers, 18, Bordesley Green.

Anti-conscription leaflet. (Political & Trade Union Archive, Jim Simmonds Papers, *vol. 2)*

influential individuals such as the union leaders W.J. Davis, John Beard, Eldred Hallas, and the women's trade union leader Julia Varley. In contrast, the Independent Labour Party (ILP) was opposed to the war and local branches organised events and talks against conscription. The Quaker artist Joseph Southall, who lived in Edgbaston, was chair of the Birmingham branch of the ILP. In March 1916, Southall spoke to the Erdington branch on the 'Futility of War', and in July a joint rally with the No Conscription Fellowship was held at the home of the Quaker and ILP supporter Henry Lloyd Wilson at Bournville, where 1,200 reportedly turned up. Joseph Southall turned his creative energies towards promoting peace and produced powerful anti-war drawings and cartoons that were published in periodicals and in polemical books and pamphlets. The images reproduced here come from his pamphlet *Fables and Illustrations* and *The Ghosts of the Slain*, which included a text written by the MP R.L. Outhwaite.[16]

Satirical illustration from Fables and Illustrations *by Joseph Southall, 1918, which echoes the recruitment poster on page 19.*

Illustration from
The Ghosts of
the Slain *by Joseph
Southall, 1915.*

The Russian Revolution had a huge impact on Birmingham's left as it did elsewhere. Nationally, the Independent Labour Party and the British Socialist Party called a conference at Leeds on 3 June 1917 to 'respond to the Russian government's call for peace' based on working-class solidarity.[17] The Leeds conference was attended by 1,150 delegates from trade unions, trades councils and local labour parties, socialist parties, and women's organisations. It proposed the establishment of Workers' and Soldiers' Councils across Britain on a Russian model. In Birmingham the proposed Workers and Soldiers Council was organised by a disabled former serviceman, Jim Simmons. Jim was born in Moseley into a family of Primitive Methodists and became a lay preacher aged 16. He enlisted in the Worcester Regiment to prove that he wasn't a coward and served in France where he was wounded in March 1915. Whilst he was recuperating he preached in public meetings against the war and in favour of peace, before rejoining his unit and serving in Gallipoli, Egypt and on the Western Front. In May 1916 he was wounded at Vimy Ridge and his lower leg was later amputated. On returning home Jim became prominent in ILP anti-war campaigns.

Jim planned the Birmingham Workers' and Soldiers' Council meeting for 18 August 1917, but it caused huge controversy locally. In a meeting of the city council, Alderman Lovsey called for it to be banned and referred to the organisers as 'a traitorous body of men – he could not call them Britishers' who were 'a disgrace to the nation'.[18] The same council meeting passed a resolution supporting the removal of the right to vote from Conscientious Objectors. On 15 August, Jim received a letter signed by the Lord Mayor David Brooks and Chief Constable Rafter, banning the meeting under the Defence of the Realm Act as they feared it would 'give rise to grave disorder'.[19] Jim Simmons did not give up; he continued his campaigning and was arrested and imprisoned for his beliefs. He was formally discharged from the army in November 1917 after which he continued his peace campaigning as 'Ex-Private Simmons'. After the war he stood as a Labour candidate in local elections.

In Spring 1918, Birmingham was shocked by the sentencing of Harrison Barrow, local businessman, Justice of the Peace, and city councillor, to six months' hard labour in Pentonville Prison. Born in 1868, Harrison was a Quaker and the son of former Lord Mayor Richard Cadbury Barrow and his wife Jane. In late May 1918, he stood trial in London's Guildhall with two other members of the Society of Friends, Arthur Watts and Edith Ellis, for refusing to submit a pamphlet *A Challenge to Militarism* to the censor before publication as required under the Defence of the Realm Act. The pamphlet described the stance taken by conscientious objectors and their imprisonment, and had been published by the Friends Service Committee of which he was chairman. On 24 May the two men were sentenced to six months' imprisonment and Ellis was awarded a fine of £100 plus costs (she later served three months after refusing to pay).

The *Birmingham Post* was outraged. In a lead article it referred to the surprise of many Birmingham citizens that such an 'estimable' man should have acted in this way, and commented that since the 'peculiar views he holds as regards war' had led him to 'such a grievous course, then he ought to be prepared to endure any penalties it may impose upon him'. They also reminded their readers that, in 1914, Harrison had been a nominee for the role of lord mayor, but had withdrawn as he felt he could not in all conscience perform the necessary military duties. The editors now suggested that 'Mr. Barrow should in his wisdom consider the desirability of withdrawing from all public activities while the war lasts'.[20] He resigned as a councillor and from his role as Chairman of the Executive of the Citizens' Committee. At his appeal hearing on 3 July 1918, Harrison conducted his own defence and argued for religious liberty of conscience and freedom of speech, even in time of war:

The Defence of the Realm Act became law on 8 August 1914 and was extended as the war progressed. It enabled the government to prosecute anyone deemed to be a danger to the course of the war and included provisions for press censorship and regulating freedom of movement.

It is said that in war time, we must submit to any curtailment of our liberties; but Truth can only be found by free discussion, and in matters of opinion, freedom, even in war time, must be preserved ... While so many thousands of men are giving their lives in the conviction that they are fighting the German idea of the worship of the State as a god, are we to do honour to that very same idol in our own homes? ... I plead for our religious liberties which have been and are a priceless possession, that all men should be free to express their ideas of truth, and to contribute each his own share to the forming of a vision that will be the salvation of the peoples.[21]

The appeal was dismissed and Harrison Barrow went to prison.

Endnotes

1   *Birmingham Daily Mail*, 9 December 1916.
2   *Birmingham Post*, 23 January 1917, p. 4.
3   MS 978.
4   MS 978, *Birmingham Daily Mail*, 16 April 1917.
5   *Towards Permanent Peace: A Record of the Women's International Congress held at The Hague, April 28th – May 1st 1915* (London: WILPF, 1915) British Library.
6   *Birmingham Gazette*, Monday, 30 July 1917, p. 3.
7   MS 466/1/1/15/3/11.
8   MS 466/1/1/15/3/46.
9   Laurence Cadbury Papers, Cadbury Research Library, University of Birmingham.
10 MS 4039.
11 MS 4039.
12 *Birmingham Weekly Mercury*, 15 April 1916, p. 3.
13 *The Friend*, 17 November 1916, p. 906.
14 MS 536/17.
15 S192/3/1.
16 Joseph Southall, *Fables and Illustrations* (London: National Labour Press, 1918) Birmingham Misc. G3/273628; R.L. Outhwaite, *The Ghosts of the Slain,* with drawings by Joseph Southall (Manchester: National Labour Press, 1915) A096/1915.
17 Quoted in Barnsby, p. 211.
18 *Birmingham Post*, 1 August 1917, p. 2.
19 Political & Trade Union Archive, Jim Simmons Papers, vol. 4.
20 *Birmingham Post*, 25 May 1918, p. 6.
21 *The Friend*, 12 July 1918, p. 443.

6

Peace and Aftermath

The last year of the war opened in Birmingham with efforts to raise money in support of it and maintain public morale after three and half years of conflict. Birmingham had already made substantial efforts towards the financing of the war, raising money to put at the disposal of the government. In addition to various flag days and other activities to raise money for the wounded, prisoners of war and other welfare appeals, the city also contributed to raising money for war loans in 1914, 1915 and 1917. One of the most significant innovations in this respect was the establishment of the Birmingham Municipal Bank, the first municipal bank in the country. It was formed at the instigation of Neville Chamberlain, who was apparently struck by the idea when walking across Chamberlain Place one day during his lord mayoralty in 1915. The city council faced strong opposition from the Treasury and from existing banks when it proposed the scheme, but finally succeeded in obtaining the necessary permission from parliament. The Municipal Bank opened on 29 September 1916 in the basement of the Corporation water department. It was heralded as an opportunity for the working classes to save and a very active campaign was conducted locally to persuade people to invest. Meetings were held in local factories, workplaces and clubs with most members subscribing sixpence a week. A prize scheme was also introduced with the award of the prizes deferred until the end of the war. Within little more than a year there were 362 associations with a membership of 45,000 people subscribing about £20,000 per month. Schools had schemes for children to subscribe. Twenty months after its formation it had 30,000 depositors who had saved £500,000 and 80 per cent of this money was lent to the government to support the cost of the war. An Act of Parliament in July 1919 ensured the bank's future as a permanent part of the city's financial scene and Neville Chamberlain laid the foundation stone of its new headquarters in Broad Street in October 1932.

From 31 December 1917 to 5 January 1918, Birmingham celebrated Tank Bank Week. An actual tank was placed outside the Town Hall to draw in the crowds, playing to the public's desire to see this new technology of the war. A civic competitive spirit came into play and Birmingham was keen to outdo other cities that had already held similar events,

Birmingham Tank Bank Week showing the running totals of Birmingham and other cities, 1918. (MS 2724)

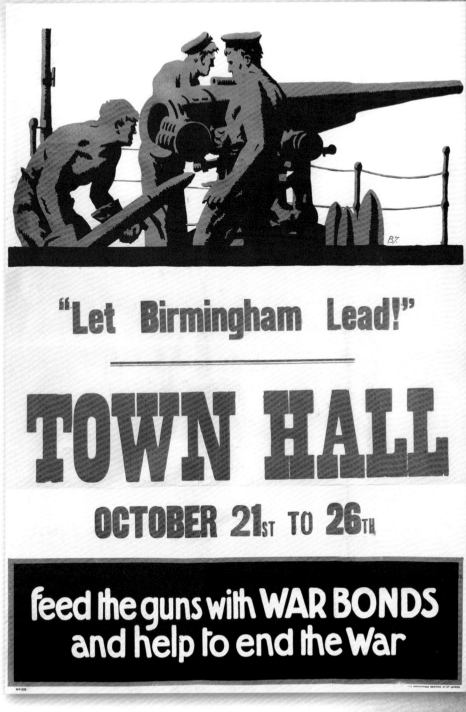

Poster for Birmingham's Big Gun Week, 1918. (LF75.7/532210)

and in particular to collect more money than Manchester and Liverpool which had raised £4,450,020 and £2,060,512 respectively. A huge board was erected at the side of the Town Hall on which the daily totals were displayed with the message 'Birmingham Must Win', and a variety of events and speeches were held in the square every day. The grand total in Birmingham, once postal deposits had been included in the count, was £6,703,439.

A few weeks later the city held Dreadnought Week from 4 to 9 March to raise £2,500,000, which was the equivalent cost

Poster for Birmingham's Big Gun Week, 1918. (LF75.7/532210)

of a dreadnought battleship. A German plane was exhibited in Victoria Square and a total of £2,710,975 was raised. Only weeks before the war came to an end, the city celebrated 'Big Gun Week' between 21 and 26 October. A replica battlefield scene was constructed in Victoria Square complete with six large guns drawn by caterpillar tractors. People were asked to feed the guns by donating money towards the cost of maintaining the supply of munitions and £7,212,204 was raised.

Even at a time when the outcome of the war was far from certain, the leading citizens of Birmingham were looking to the future and to post-war regeneration. At a meeting in the Council House on 10 June, Neville Chamberlain moved a resolution to found a Civic Society for the city, a proposal seconded by George Cadbury Junior. They were supported by a whole range of influential and well-known local dignitaries, or in the words of the society's first report, 'Birmingham Citizens who see the necessity of stimulating a wider concern for the beauty of their city.'[1] The Civic Society went on to take a prominent role in lobbying to improve the city's buildings, parks and open spaces, and to preserve historical buildings. It also took a leading role in the plans to provide a suitable war memorial for the city.

Birmingham's industrial contribution to the war was celebrated with the Birmingham 'Win the War Day' on 21 September 1918. The local press described the aims of the day as 'to bring forth to the people the magnitude of the city's efforts to win the war, to stimulate the active to additional exertion, and to enlist the services of those who are at the moment not doing any "national work"'. A procession of floats 2 miles long, representing local manufacturers and organisations illustrating the city's war work, wound its way through the city centre and out to Cannon Hill Park. Great interest was caused by the American troops of 1st and 2nd Battalions of the 335th Regiment of Infantry (known as the 'Lincolns') who had arrived in Birmingham on Saturday morning and marched alongside the 'Old Contemptibles', discharged soldiers, many wearing the Mons ribbon and displaying the motto 'How to be

Happy though Crocked', the Royal Warwicks, Home Defence Volunteers and the Cadets including 'some very small boys' for whom the crowd showed their appreciation. The parade of women workers, some in uniform and many on lorries, was also popular with the crowd, and they were joined by VADs, WVR, the Land Army and Girl Guides.[2]

Less than two months later, peace was declared. On 11 November 1918, the city went to work as usual but a few minutes before 11 a.m. the pre-arranged maroons (fireworks) signalled the Armistice and work and business were suspended. The rest of the day was spent as a general holiday to mark the occasion, although for many it was a celebration tinged with sadness and loss. A crowd gathered in Victoria Square and were addressed by the lord mayor, Sir David Brooks, who looked to the future:

6,146,574 British men served and 740,000 died. Death rates for the Empire as a whole were 908,000. Losses in other combatant nations were even higher:

Austria-Hungary – 7.8 million fought, 1.2 million died
Germany – 11 million fought, 1.8 million died
France – 8.4 million fought, 1.4 million died
Russia – 12 million fought, 1.7 million died

To-day is the greatest day in the history of our country, and it marks the beginning of a new era in human development. We can hardly realise that the war has ended … We must take care to use this great opportunity aright, so that the world may be better and not worse by reason of the overthrow of the old order. In following this sacred duty we must never forget those who have died and suffered in order that justice might be vindicated, liberty established, and peace made secure. This means that we must think of our duties and responsibilities before our own rights and privileges, so that each may play a worthy part in the great work of reconstruction and regeneration that lies before us.[3]

A thanksgiving service was held at St Philip's Cathedral at 12 p.m. So many people wished to attend that a large crowd congregated outside in the churchyard and the service had to be held three times. A number of events occurred across the city, with bands parading the streets and evening gatherings held in local parks where the occasion was marked by displays of fireworks. Bonfires were lit on Barr Beacon and the Lickey Hills.[4] Schoolchildren were also given a holiday. At City Road School the maroon went at 10.40 a.m. and the children assembled in the yard where they had cheers and sang patriotic songs. The school was dismissed until Wednesday when children returned to school, but the head teacher recorded that they were 'much too overjoyed & unsettled to concentrate on school work' a feeling which continued all week.[5]

Kynoch float at the Birmingham Win the War Day, 1918. (MS 1422/1)

Avery's Boy Scout troop parading at the Birmingham Win the War Day, 1918. (MS 4616/6)

Avery's parade of women workers at the Birmingham Win the War Day, 1918. (MS 4616/6)

Avery float at the Birmingham Win the War Day Parade, 1918. (MS 4616/6)

Victory celebrations at Bordesley Green School, 1918. (MS 1645/14)

The celebrations lasted for days. On 14 November the local press was reporting that although some people had returned to work, generally 'holiday-makers' outnumbered the workers, and the previous evening had seen crowds in The Square, New Street and Corporation Street, who were singing, waving flags, 'turkey-trotting' and 'bunny-hugging' – two popular ragtime dances of the period.[6] The 15 November saw a Military Investiture in Victoria Square where the lord mayor presented military decorations to about 100 servicemen. The troops attending included detachments of Warwickshire Volunteer Regiment, the Federation of Discharged and Demobilised Soldiers and Sailors, The Old Contemptibles 'who came in for a great cheer', the Warwickshire cadets and the cadets of Norton Boys Home.[7]

Once the initial relief and celebrations were over thoughts turned to dealing with some of the issues that came with peace. Many of the thousands of munition workers in the city were soon unemployed as the firms that had expanded their workforce for the war effort wound down. There were 'animated scenes' on Friday, 3 January 1919 at the Central Employment Exchange in Corporation Street as discharged women workers queued for hours to register for the dole. The men were dealt with at Woodcock Street Baths but the local press reported that 'the women considerably outnumber the men' and concluded that 'it is obvious that a very large proportion of the workers who have left the munition factories are still on the unemployment list'.[8] There were so many workers registering for unemployment that a few days later Curzon Hall, and Kent Street, Nechells and Monument Lane Baths were pressed into service as temporary labour exchanges and extra clerical staff was brought in to try and alleviate the queues.[9]

The war is often credited with changing the position of women in society but in fact many of the gains made by women were short term. As men were demobilised from the armed services it was assumed that women would 'naturally' return to a domestic role of wife and mother. Women did receive the right to vote towards the end of the war in the Representation of the People Act 1918, which also extended the vote to working-class men who had previously been excluded. *Women Workers,* the magazine of Birmingham's National Union of Women Workers, celebrated the news with the words 'At Last!' heading an article by veteran local suffragist Catherine Osler. She summarised the long campaign women had fought over the previous sixty years to reach this point, but also drew attention to the fact that women still could not vote on the same terms as men. The suffrage was limited to women over the age of 30 who fulfilled a residential qualification. As Osler stated, 'It leaves still unrepresented classes of women who are among the worthiest, most indispensable workers for their country and their fellows', not least of course all the young women under 30 who had flocked to the munition works or undertaken war work as VADs.[10] They had to wait another ten years.

The immediate post-war period also saw increasing industrial strife as a number of strikes disrupted the city. The war years had been relatively strike-free as the trade unions had agreed to forgo industrial action. Despite this, 1917 and early 1918 had seen some industrial unrest including a strike in January 1918 at the Austin Works in Longbridge. January 1919 began with another disagreement between the workers and management at Longbridge about the reorganisation of working patterns under the agreement for the adoption of a forty-seven-hour week.[11] In the summer the police force went on strike and, in a highly acrimonious dispute, three sergeants, 116 constables, and at least three prison officers from Winson Green were dismissed from their posts that September for striking. September also saw local ironfounders come out on strike and remain out until the end of January 1920. In the same period, the city's rail services came to a halt during a lengthy railway strike.

Most of the men who had served in the armed forces were demobilised between January and April 1919 but for many the return home was fraught with difficulty. Ex-servicemen had begun organising politically on their own behalf during the war, and associations were formed to campaign for better conditions for the veterans. In 1919 the socialist National Union of Ex-Servicemen was formed, with Charles Leatherland as a leading local organiser. Leatherland had served in the 3rd City Battalion in which he had enlisted at the age of 16. After the war he wrote a weekly column in the *Town Crier*, the newspaper of Birmingham's labour movement, where he articulated the ex-servicemen's grievances and lobbied for improved conditions. In May 1919, the Birmingham branch of the National Federation of Discharged and Demobilised Sailors and Soldiers held a large protest meeting of local ex-servicemen at the Hippodrome. The building was crowded as Labour Councillor Tiptaft presided over a mass meeting which called for increased payments for those who had served their country.[12] By the end of 1919 the local branches of the National Union of Ex-Servicemen were protesting against the city's proposed war memorial arguing that the money should be spent on housing for ex-servicemen.

Ex-servicemen's organisations:

- National Association of Discharged Sailors and Soldiers, 1916
- National Federation of Discharged and Demobilised Sailors and Soldiers, 1917
- Comrades of the Great War, 1917
- National Union of Ex-Servicemen, 1919

The NADSS, NFDDSS, Comrades of the Great War, and Officers Association merged to form the British Legion, 1921.

THE HEROES' REWARD.

1

The Wealthy of England, they promised a land
  "Fit for Heroes to live in."   Oh lor! ain't it grand!
"Rare and Refreshing" should be all the fruit,
  But Heroes find NOW that this stunt doesn't suit!
They gave of their best, that their homes might be brighter,
  But NOW they can starve—whilst the Wealthy sit tighter!

2

The Wealthy of England are hunting the foxes—
  The Heroes of England are shaking their boxes.
The Wealthy of England draw millions in rents—
  The Heroes of England are begging for cents.
They fought for "THEIR" Country, in glorious belief—
  But NOW, in their thousands, apply for relief!

You've been "Had" ONCE —
Don't be "Had again"!

THIS TIME

To Secure Justice—

VOTE for SIMMONS,

The LABOUR PARTY CANDIDATE.

Printed and Published by J. Patrick, Pershore-st., Birmingham.

Election leaflet of Jim Simmonds appealing particularly to disillusioned ex-servicemen, c. 1919.
(Political & Trade Union Archive, Jim Simmonds Papers, vol. 2)

A pamphlet published in Birmingham in 1920 summarises their grievances. 'The Case for the Ex-Serviceman' was written by Captain E.C. Whillier, the chairman of a local joint committee of the National Federation and another ex-servicemen's organisation called the Comrades of the Great War. The text was based on a series of lectures that he delivered to ex-servicemen in the city in autumn 1920. The cover was illustrated with a dramatic image of an ex-serviceman bound in chains in front of a 'fat cat' businessman and a woman socialite carrying a large bag of money. It was subtitled 'Spurned, Betrayed, Bereft'. All the proceeds of the pamphlet were 'devoted to the relief of hardship, want, and destitution amongst Ex-Service men, their dependants, and the dependants of our gallant Comrades who have made the Supreme Sacrifice'. Whillier argued that although servicemen had been promised a country fit for heroes, none of the promises had been kept. He maintained that of the 16,000 unemployed men in Birmingham, ex-servicemen comprised over half, and that all the jobs worth having were taken by men who had stayed at home furthering their careers whilst the ex-servicemen were at the front. In relation to the housing shortage he argued that 'Germans, Belgians and Chinese occupy houses, but the Ex-Service man can house his family in the Workhouse'. He demanded an Act of Parliament that would give preference to ex-servicemen in employment, government appointments and housing, and better unemployment pay and disability pensions.[13]

Many of the ex-servicemen came home with physical and psychological scars. From as early as 1915, the Citizens' Committee had turned its attention to wounded discharged soldiers and co-ordinated the efforts of various local charitable and welfare initiatives such as the technical schools, the schools for the blind and the deaf, and the YMCA to provide training for rehabilitation into work, and to assist if further medical attention was required. In the first months of 1918 there were over 13,000 discharged soldiers returning to the city, and in February alone 650 of those applied for assistance with further medical treatment. Large amounts of money were raised locally for homes and hospitals for disabled soldiers, initially for the Star

Poster encouraging local firms to employ disabled ex-servicemen, c. 1919. (MS 4383)

and Garter Home at Richmond. Later initiatives collected for providing a home in Birmingham itself and £4,148 was collected for this purpose during Neville Chamberlain's lord mayoralty. Austen Chamberlain gave Highbury for the treatment of disabled soldiers and sailors, and money was raised to buy the adjoining land and for the adaptation of the buildings. Over £40,000 had been raised by the beginning of 1920. From September 1918, Uffculme was a specialist centre for treating men who had lost limbs, and later became a home for disabled ex-servicemen. Sorrento in Wake Green was acquired by the War Pensions Committee as a hospital for paraplegic pensioners.

A committee for the training of disabled men was established in Birmingham by the local War Pensions Committee, this included representatives from the major firms of the city among others. Training classes were held in a number of local educational establishments including the Municipal Technical School, the technical schools in Aston, Handsworth and Erdington, and the School of Art in Margaret Street. Instructional factories were established at Lancaster Street and Garrison Lane. In December 1919, the city council's Distress Committee discussed a report on unemployment in the city, at a point when the unemployed comprised of 10,191 men, 2,745 women, 146 boys, and 118 girls, a total of 13,200 people. The committee heard that of the unemployed men the proportion of ex-servicemen to civilians was about four to one. Approximately 6,000 were demobilised soldiers and a further 2,000 were soldiers who were disabled in some way, 1,000 of whom were receiving training under government schemes as bricklayers, carpenters, plumbers, painters and plasterers in the hope that they would find employment in the building trade. Employers were supposed to ensure that 5 per cent of their workforce was made up of disabled men but the results locally were disappointing.

The problem was aggravated by the fact that a large number of the unemployed ex-servicemen had no training or experience to fit them for employment, as the committee explained they 'were boys on joining the Army, in many cases having given fictitious ages to enable them to join, and the position now was that after having served the country they were without a trade or employ-ment'. Mr Dalley of the Employment Exchange argued that the only chance to absorb these men was to train them for a trade. With regards to women, the committee was informed that 'there were a number of Domestic Servants who went into Munition factories, and who could not now be prevailed upon to go back to domestic service' but the Employment Exchanges were gradually placing them in employment. The committee resolved to send representations to the government urging the need for training in a trade for demobilised unemployed men on the same basis as the disabled men, and further that all employers should be reminded of the need to employ the 5 per cent quota of disabled men.[14]

Psychological disabilities were less visible but had equally long-term consequences for the individual men and their fami-lies. Over ten years after the end of the war, a coroner's inquest on the death of George Henry Bonner illustrates the often-hidden story of the men who came back suffering. George was a 33-year-old journalist when he died on 2 March 1929 and lived with his mother and wife at No. 31 Radnor Road, Handsworth.

Disabled employees at Cadbury's Works, Bournville, 1925. (MS 466/50/192)

He had served with the army in France and was discharged with shell shock in 1919. In her evidence to the inquest, his mother, Margaret Elizabeth Bonner, testified that he had 'suffered with it more or less ever since'. She described how he 'suffered very badly with pains in his head and [blood] pressure, and could not sleep. When he had a bad attack of Shell Shock he would stay in bed for a couple of days but would not have medical attention.' George had suffered a recurrence of his condition over the previous fortnight, he had several sleepless nights, 'seemed very depressed' and the doctor was called. On the afternoon of Saturday, 2 March, his wife took him for a walk, but after only a few yards he had a bad attack of shivering and had to return home. They managed to get him to his bedroom and the doctor was called again. George went to his study saying he wished to be left alone. Two friends came to see him in the evening but when they knocked on his study door there was no answer. When they forced the door they discovered that George had hanged himself from the casement window. He left no letter or note explaining his actions.[15] Although we have no statistics for how many men in Birmingham suffered as George did, his family were one of many who had to live for years with the psychological legacy of the conflict.

The war's international legacy was of concern to a number of Birmingham citizens who were very concerned about civilian distress in Europe, particularly the effect that the continuing Allied sea blockade was having on women and children in Austria. There was a tradition of involvement in humanitarian aid in Europe during the war, particularly among members of the local Quaker community. Several Birmingham Quakers had left for Europe as relief workers under the auspices of the Friends War Victims Relief Committee. One of the most active Quakers during and after the war was Florence Barrow who was born in Birmingham in 1876, the daughter of Richard Cadbury Barrow and his wife Jane, and the sister of Harrison Barrow. Florence had a background in adult

'Shell shock' or neurasthenia was first described by Charles Myers in a 1915 article in *The Lancet*. Men suffering with the condition were often suspected of malingering or cowardice. By the end of the war military hospitals had treated 80,000 men suffering with the condition.

education for women and in welfare work with the Birmingham Women's Settlement in Summer Lane. Soon after the outbreak of war she left for France where she worked with Serbian refugees in a quarantine station near Marseille. In 1916 she moved to Buzuluk in Russia where she was involved in feeding programmes, establishing nurseries for children and occupational workshops. Florence and another Birmingham Quaker, Annie R. Wells, were both in Russia during the Revolution in 1917. In later recollections of her work in Russia, she gave an insight into what motivated her to undertake this difficult and dangerous work so far from home:

> Before deciding exactly what form our relief work should take many hundreds of families of refugees were visited. I do not know that I ever have had a sadder & more depressing piece of work. To go into house after house & find old men, women, girls, children sitting inert unoccupied & hopeless, unwelcome guests in an already overcrowded home. One after another would tell of the good house they had left in the west surrounded by a pleasant fruitful garden ... Nevertheless we are convinced that the sufferings these people have undergone & are undergoing has a special claim upon us whose homes have not been destroyed by war or who have not been transported as unwelcome guests into districts 1000's of miles away there to drag out year after year a dreary & miserable existence.[16]

Florence returned to Birmingham in July 1918, but a few months later, in 1919, she was part of a Quaker team undertaking relief and famine work with women and children in defeated Germany, where food was in very short supply. Writing from Breslau she described how doctors 'showed us one tiny distorted form after another it was almost more than one could bear'.[17] She then moved to Poland where she led the Quaker relief team until 1924, providing food, medical help, housing, agricultural implements and seeds, and establishing orphanages and schools for children.

OUR BLINDED HEROES

LORD MAYOR'S FUND
FOR BLINDED SOLDIERS, Etc.

They have given their Sight for you.

WILL YOU HELP TO LIGHTEN THEIR DARKNESS ?

Poster fundraising for the Lord Mayor's Fund for Blinded Soldiers, c. 1918. (S256/21/6)

The girls from Vienna with George and Elizabeth Cadbury at the Manor House, 1921. (MS 466/8/53)

On her return home in 1924, Florence threw herself into housing reform and was instrumental in the founding of the Copec Housing Improvement Society. She returned to relief work in the 1930s working with refugees in Syria, Salonika and Egypt, before returning to Germany and Austria in the late 1930s to assist Jews.

Reports of the widespread famine affecting women and children in central Europe were sent home by relief workers like Florence in 1918–19 and resulted in the establishment of the Lord Mayor's European Famine Fund. A similar motivation led to the arrival of eighteen girls from Vienna in Bournville on 29 October 1920. *The Friend* reported their arrival, describing them as 'sweet-looking children of from 8 to 12 years of age [who] all appeared to be very happy as they trooped into the Infants' School, many of them carrying all their possessions in a small bundle on their backs'.[18] The girls lived with local families for a year and returned to Vienna on 2 September 1921 when *The Friend* contrasted their 'healthy, plump looking' appearance with the 'thin, emaciated and badly clothed' children who had arrived a year earlier.[19]

Endnotes

1   Report of Birmingham Civic Society, 1918–20, L20.53/285809.
2   *Birmingham Post*, 23 September 1918, p. 8.
3   Quoted in Brazier and Sandford, p. 338.
4   *Birmingham Post*, 11 November 1918, p. 6.
5   S48/1/1.
6   *Birmingham Post*, 14 November 1918, p. 7.
7   *Birmingham Post*, 16 November 1918, p. 10.
8   *Birmingham Post*, 4 January 1919, p. 8.
9   *Birmingham Post*, 6 January 1919, p. 8.
10 *Women Workers*, March 1918, pp. 95–9.
11 *Birmingham Post*, 4 January 1919, p. 10.
12 *Birmingham Post*, 19 May 1919, p. 8.
13 Birmingham Institutions C21/294503.
14 Minutes BCC 1/BJ/1/1/1.
15 Coroner's Inquest, 4 March 1929.
16 Recollections of work in Buzuluk, The Friends Library, London,
    Temp MSS 590/1.
17 Quoted in Oldfield, p. 17.
18 *The Friend*, 19 November 1920, p. 743
19 *The Friend*, 16 September 1921, p. 613.

Lord Mayor's European Famine Fund

In December 1919, Birmingham's lord mayor, William Adlington Cadbury, founded the Lord Mayor's European Famine Fund at the behest of some of the city's leading citizens. It was a multi-faith group including members of the Church of England, the Jewish community, Nonconformist ministers, and Quakers. The Famine Fund raised money and collected clothes and other goods to send to Austria. They worked closely with the Save the Children Fund, founded in May 1919 in response to the distress in Europe, and with the Quaker Relief Mission in Vienna led by Dr Hilda Clark. Clark had close connections to Birmingham; the granddaughter of John Bright, she trained in medicine here before working briefly at Birmingham Maternity Hospital. Her aunt, Dr Annie Clark, was one of Birmingham's first women medical practitioners. Bertha Bracey and Constance Smith from Bournville worked with Clark in Vienna in the early 1920s, establishing feeding depots and medical treatment centres for children.

The Lord Mayor's Fund raised £30,058 over a period of two years. Although most of the activity was centred on Austria, and on the Tyrol in particular, it also supported relief work in Armenia, Hungary, Poland, Serbia and Russia. The money was raised by public subscription, local churches and synagogues, political and charitable organisations and schools. Over £2,000 was raised by schoolchildren in Birmingham to help the children of Austria. The Lord Mayor's Fund paid for a children's home called the Birmingham and District Famine Home for Children (or 'Kinderheim') in Kitzbuhel. The home opened in June 1920 and by autumn 1920 over 145 children from Innsbruck and Vienna were living there. The Lord Mayor's Fund was closed in October 1921 when the committee decided to concentrate on helping the poor of Birmingham, which by that time was suffering from high unemployment.

BIRMINGHAM & DISTRICT KINDERHEIM.

" Home and country are but names made sweet
By their promise of a love complete,
When, as brothers, all the nations meet "

W.A. Cadbury

Kitzbühel-Innsbruck.
1920-1921.

Promotional leaflet for the Austrian children's home funded by the Lord Mayor's European Famine Fund, 1920–21. (MS 3241/2)

MOURNING AND MEMORIALS

'Never mind if you feel a prig & if you look a fool before the rest of the world those living in 2016 will be the best judges of whether you did right or wrong at this time.'

Gerald Lloyd, February 1916.[1]

The First World War had a profound impact on individuals and families across the city. The human cost of the war in terms of lives lost, or changed forever by physical and psychological scars, was on an almost inconceivable scale and would cast a shadow over individual lives for decades to come. Nationally it is estimated that the war left about 240,000 widows and 350,000 orphans, as well as those husbands and fathers who returned home wounded in some way. The need for personal and collective mourning and commemoration would leave its legacy on the city's physical environment and landscape, and in its collections.

Within a year the city was celebrating the signing of the peace treaty. A 'Pageant of Peace' was held in Cannon Hill Park from 9–14 June 1919, written and directed by Pageant Master Leolyn Hart and performed by the citizens of Birmingham. All the proceeds went to the Blinded Soldiers and Sailors After-care Fund. The pageant was a huge affair made up of six tableau, beginning with a representation of 'Empire at Peace', and including depictions of Belgian refugees, the Old Contemptibles embarking for France, 'The Great Retreat' where two gun teams galloped across the arena, and groups of exhausted soldiers represented the 'fight to the last'. 'Heroes All' included a depiction of the scenes in which Turrall, Vickers and Finch won their Victoria Crosses. The pageant closed with a tableau showing the 'Spirit of Peace' on a pedestal with the 'Demon of War' at her feet, crushed and destroyed.[2]

On Saturday, 19 July 1919, the city was decked in flags for the official civic celebrations, and crowds thronged the main squares and streets of the city, dressed in the national colours of the allies and banging home-made drums and what the press referred to as other improvised 'unmusical instruments'. Even the heavy rain didn't dampen the enthusiasm. Theatres and cinemas were crowded and the public houses did a roaring trade whilst supplies held out. Entertainment was provided in parks across the city for schoolchildren, many in costumes. At Cannon Hill Park 8,000 attended the festivities whilst at Ward End Park there were 10,000 children in attendance and Aston Park catered for over 13,000.[3] The children of City Road School were among the 12,000 assembled in Summerfield Park

Children on a Birmingham Co-operative Society float at the May Day Parade, 1920. (MS 4616/1)

Peace Medal given to Birmingham schoolchildren to mark the signing of the peace treaty, 1919. (MS 4034/4)

and like all other schoolchildren in the city they each received a Birmingham peace medal to commemorate the occasion. They were then treated to a special tea at the school and had an extra week added to their summer holiday, in the words of the head teacher 'to celebrate a Victorious Peace'.[4]

The Hall of Memory bronze statues depicting the army and the air force being cast in the foundry. (MS 2724/Hall of Memory/34)

Discussions had begun during the war about what form the permanent war memorial should take. The compilation of the names of the fallen was initiated by Alderman Bowater when he took over as lord mayor in 1914 and recorded in the Lord Mayor's Parlour. It was originally planned to establish a War Memorial Museum, and in October 1917 the city council set up a committee to investigate the matter. In 1919,

Sir Whitworth Wallis, the keeper of the Birmingham Museum and Art Gallery, presented a report that proposed establishing a museum incorporating a Hall of Honour, or Hall of Memory, in Cannon Hill Park to provide a permanent home for the Roll of Honour. However, the Birmingham Civic Society argued that the memorial should be in the city centre and occupy a green space laid out with grass and trees around a Hall of Memory. The museum scheme was abandoned. In November 1921, the architects S.N. Cooke and W.N. Twist won the competition to design the Hall of Memory, and the foundation stone was laid by the Prince of Wales on 12 June 1923.[5]

The Roll of Honour itself was designed by Sidney H. Meteyard of the Birmingham Central School of Art, and written and illuminated by Kate M. Eadie of the Royal Miniature Society. The Hall of Memory was opened on 4 July 1925 by Price Arthur of Connaught. The official programme for the opening described the hall as 'a "temple of tender memory" of those who are gone', and a 'shrine in enduring stone' in Birmingham to those whose graves were scattered across the world.[6] Bronze statues by Albert Toft sit at its four corners, symbolising the parts played by the army, the navy and the air force in the war, with the fourth, female figure representing the role played by women. The stained glass was designed by R.J. Stubington and inside are the powerful relief carvings by William Bloye, symbolising three elements of the war. The first shows men leaving home to join the forces over the inscription 'Of 150,000 who answered the call to arms, 12,320 fell: 35,000 came home disabled'. The second shows men in battle accompanied by the inscription 'At the going down of the sun and in the morning we will remember them'. The third depicts the return of the wounded with the words 'See to it that they shall not have suffered and died in vain'.

A number of societies and organisations across the city instigated their own memorials and they are to be found cast in metal or stone at churches, schools, factories, train stations and other public spaces across the city. In addition to these formal collective memorials, many individuals and families inaugurated their own personal tributes and rituals of mourning.

The opening of Birmingham Hall of Memory, 4 July 1925. (MS 2724/Hall of Memory/48)

In 1921 Birmingham Library was presented with a collection of poetry originally donated anonymously in memory of William John Billington who was killed in action in Palestine in March 1918. The donor was William John Cross of Rubery who had amassed a collection of 1,233 books and pamphlets of poetry from the First World War, written by both soldiers and civilians, some well known others less so. Many of the items in the collection were printed privately by families in memory of sons or brothers. One such was Thomas Ewart Mitton – known as Ewart to his family – a former pupil of King Edward's School in Birmingham and a member of a prosperous family from Moseley. After school he enlisted in the Royal Engineers. He went to France in March 1917 and was then transferred to Belgium. Ewart was killed on Christmas Eve 1917 near Ypres aged 20.

The family of Henry Lionel Field published his poems and sketches in 1917. Harry, as he was known in the family, was a

Bookplate from the Library of Birmingham's War Poetry Collection.

former student at Marlborough and Birmingham School of Art and served in the 6th Battalion of the Royal Warwickshire Regiment. He was killed in action on the first day of the Somme on 1 July 1916.[7] In the foreword to the book, his mother Ruth described her purpose in printing the small volume: 'that people who care for him, and for whom this book is intended, may see and know something of his inner life during the arduous years of learning and training, up to the great attack on 1 July.' Similarly, in 1920 the parents of Cristian Creswell Carver published his correspondence for private circulation among the family, as the foreword states they were 'letters so anxiously looked out for, so eagerly welcomed'.[8]

Families who were not as affluent often kept a small collection of family papers. Taking a family photograph with the son or father in uniform before he departed for the front had become a ritual for many families. Postcards were popular as a quick and easy means of communication and many families treasured service postcards and letters from the front. Many of these collections have found their way into the archives of the Library of Birmingham and form another collective testimony to the city's past.

Archives are fundamentally about people; the people who created them at the time, and those who read them a century later. In compiling this short study I have used the archive collections to try and reflect the motivations and experiences of a range of people in Birmingham during the First World War. It has inevitably been shaped by my choices of stories and selections from the archive, and another author may well have taken a different approach. Many stories and voices remain to be uncovered in the Library of Birmingham's collections. It is only by engaging with them that we can respond to the challenge posed by Gerald Lloyd at the beginning of this postscript.

Endnotes

1   MS 4039.
2   Official Souvenir Programme 'The Pageant of Peace', June 1919, MS 4384.
3   *Birmingham Post*, 21 July 1919, p. 8.

4   S48/1/1.
5   *The Hall of Memory, Birmingham*, 668808 LP75.9; Official
    programme of the visit, 1923, Birmingham History H3/414639.
6   Souvenir and Official Programme, 4 July 1925, L22.3/41305.
7   H.L. Field, *Poems and Sketches* (Birmingham: Cornish
    Brothers, 1917) L07.3.
8   *Christian Creswell Carver* (Birmingham: Privately
    Published, 1920) L78.1, also available online at
    http://ww1centenary.oucs.ox.ac.uk/bookmark/
    christian-creswell-carver-university-of-oxford/

BIBLIOGRAPHY AND SOURCES

The literature of the First World War is vast. This bibliography therefore concentrates on works that are relevant to Birmingham, and which were used to compile this book.

Anyone wishing to find further reference works relating to Birmingham and the war should consult the catalogues to the local studies collections in the Library of Birmingham.

This book has drawn extensively on Brazier and Sandford in particular. I have also drawn on the work of Briggs, Hopkins and Barnsby, supplemented by original research in the archive and heritage collections of the Library of Birmingham.

Published Works

Barnsby, George, *Socialism in Birmingham and the Black Country 1850–1939* (Wolverhampton: Integrated Publishing Services, 1998)

Bill, Charles A., *The 15th Battalion Royal Warwickshire Regiment (2nd Birmingham Battalion) in the Great War* (Birmingham: Cornish Brothers, 1932)

Brazier, Reginald H. and Ernest Sandford, *Birmingham and the Great War 1914–1919* (Birmingham: Cornish Brothers Ltd, 1921)

Briggs, Asa, *History of Birmingham, vol. II, Borough and City 1865–1938* (London: Oxford University Press, 1952)

Cadbury Brothers, *Bournville Works and The War: A Record of the Firm's & Workers' Activities 1914–1919* (Birmingham: Cadbury Brothers, 1919)

Carter, Terry, *Birmingham Pals: A History of the Three City Battalions Raised in Birmingham in the Great War* (Barnsley: The Pen and Sword Books, 2011)

Crosfield, John F., *A History of the Cadbury Family* (Cambridge: Cambridge University Press, 1985)

Davis, Robert (ed.), *Woodbrooke 1903–1953. A Brief History of a Quaker Experiment in Religious Education* (London: The Bannisdale Press, 1953)

Frost, George, *Munitions of War: A record of the work of the B.S.A. and Daimler Companies during the World War 1914–1918* (Birmingham and Coventry: The B.S.A. Co. Ltd and Daimler Co. Ltd, 1919)

Greyzel, Susan R., *Women and the First World War* (Harlow: Pearson Education Ltd, 2002)

Hamilton, Peggy, *Three Years or the Duration: The Memoirs of a Munition Worker, 1914–1918* (London: Peter Owen, 1978)

Hilton, J.P., *Britain's First Municipal Savings Bank. The Romance of a Great Achievement* (Birmingham: Blackfriars Press Ltd, 1927)

Hopkins, Eric, *Birmingham: The Making of the Second City 1850–1939* (Stroud: Tempus Publishing Ltd, 2001)

Howard, Michael, *The First World War: A Very Short Introduction* (Oxford: Oxford University Press, 2002)

Jones, Joseph T., *History of the Corporation of Birmingham,* vol. V, part I (Birmingham: Birmingham City Council, 1940)

Kennedy, Thomas C., *British Quakerism 1860–1920: The Transformation of a Religious Community* (Oxford: Oxford University Press, 2001)

Kushner, Tony and Katherine Knox, *Refugees in an Age of Genocide: Global, National and Local Perspectives during the Twentieth Century* (London: Frank Cass, 1999)

Kynoch, *Notes on Kynoch War Work* (Birmingham: Kynoch Press, 1918)

Kynoch, *Notes on Kynoch War Work* (Birmingham: Kynoch Press, 1919)

Lethbridge, J.P., *Birmingham in the First World* War (Birmingham: Newgate Press, 1993)

Lethbridge, J.P., *Birmingham Heroes* (Birmingham: Newgate Press, 1993)

Lethbridge, J.P., *More About Birmingham in the First World* War (Birmingham: Newgate Press, 1994)

Meyer, Jessica, *Men of War: Masculinity and the First World War in Britain* (Basingstoke: Palgrave Macmillan, 2011)

Oldfield, Sybil, *Women Humanitarians: A Biographical Dictionary of British Women Active between 1900 and 1950* (London: Continuum, 2001)

Outhwaite, R.L., *The Ghosts of the Slain,* with drawings by Joseph Southall (Manchester: National Labour Press, 1915)

Simmons, Jim, *Soap-Box Evangelist* (Chichester: Janay Publishing Company, 1972)

Southall, Joseph, *Fables and Illustrations* (London: National Labour Press, 1918)

Todman, Dan, *The Great War: Myth and Memory* (London: Bloomsbury, 2005)

Trade Union Resource Centre, *The People's Century, Birmingham 1889–1989* (Birmingham: TURC Publishing Ltd, 1989)

Upton, Chris, *A History of Birmingham* (Andover: Phillimore, 1993)

Ward, Roger, *City-State and Nation: Birmingham's Political History c.1830–1940* (Chichester: Phillimore, 2005)

Walters, Florence S. (Mrs Arthur Walters), *My Wayside* (London: The Epworth Press, 1930)

Woollacott, Angela, *On Her Their Lives Depend: Munitions Workers in the Great War* (London: University of California Press, 1994)

Wiltshire, Anne, *Most Dangerous Women* (Henley: Pandora Press Ltd, 1985)

Winter, Jay and Jean-Louis Robert (eds), *Capital Cities at War: Paris, London, Berlin 1914–1919, Volume 2: A Cultural History* (Cambridge: Cambridge University Press, 2007)

Newspapers and Periodicals

Birmingham Gazette

Birmingham Mail

Birmingham Post

Birmingham Weekly Mercury

The Friend

The Manchester Guardian

The Times

Women Workers

Unpublished Sources

Judy P. Lloyd, 'The Lloyds of Birmingham: Quaker Culture and Identity 1850–1918' (PhD thesis, University College London, 2006) LoB reference MS 4039

Online Resources

Adrian Barlow, '"The Word is Said": rereading the poetry of John Drinkwater', www.johndrinkwater.org

Birmingham Pals, www.birminghampals.co.uk

British Library First World, www.bl.uk/world-war-one

Charles Edward Leatherland 1898–1992, www.charlesleatherland.info

Johnson, Mel, 'Simmons, Charles James (1893–1975)', *Oxford Dictionary of National Biography*, Oxford University Press, October 2013, www.oxforddnb.com/view/article/105625.

Killeen, Martin, 'Considerable Derangement of Civilian Life' patriotism and protest in suburban Birmingham, 1914–1918' (2010), www.suburbanbirmingham.org.uk/spaces/worldwar1-essay.htm

Quakers in Britain, www.quaker.org.uk/news/white-feather-diaries

The Long, Long Trail: The British Army in the Great War of 1914–1918, www.1914-1918.net

The Open University, The Women Police, www.open.ac.uk/Arts/history-from-police-archives/Met6Kt/WomenPolice/wpWW1.html

The Ruhleben Story, http://ruhleben.tripod.com

Tucker, Alan, 'Hellfire Corner – Diary of Capt. Arthur Impey',
with a transcript of the diary,
www.hellfirecorner.co.uk/tucker/tuckernavigation.htm
Voices of War and Peace: The Great War and its Legacy,
www.voicesofwarandpeace.org/portfolio/resources/

Oral Histories

Birmingham Museum and Art Gallery hold a collection of oral histories relating to the First World War:

R0089 Victor Woolley © Birmingham Museums Trust
R0658-9 Mrs Naughton Dunn © Birmingham Museums Trust
R0087 Edith Warwood © Birmingham Museums Trust

Some of the recordings can be found at
www.voicesofwarandpeace.org/portfolio/resources/

Archive Sources

This study has drawn from a whole range of archive collections in the Library of Birmingham including family papers, the city council's archive, business archives, and the collections relating to various organisations and institutions. Reference numbers to particular collections or documents used are given in the endnotes to each chapter. On the rare occasions that archives from collections held elsewhere have been used, this information will also be found in the endnotes.

For particular queries relating to archives of the First World War in Birmingham, contact the Library of Birmingham www.libraryofbirmingham.com.

Great War Britain:
The First World War at Home

Luci Gosling

After the declaration of war in 1914, the conflict dominated civilian life for the next four years. Magazines quickly adapted without losing their gossipy essence: fashion jostled for position with items on patriotic fundraising, and court presentations were replaced by notes on nursing. The result is a fascinating, amusing and uniquely feminine perspective of life on the home front.

978 0 7524 9188 2

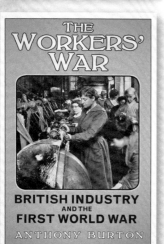

The Workers' War:
British Industry and the First World War

Anthony Burton

The First World War didn't just rock the nation in terms of bloodshed: it was a war of technological and industrial advances. Working Britain experienced change as well: with the men at war, it fell to the women of the country to keep the factories going. Anthony Burton explores that change.

978 0 7524 9886 7